Rev,
May you enjoy! Maureen ♡
I mean find it helpful

To my mother, Glenda
The woman who gave me life
A two-time breast cancer survivor

To my husband, Chris
Whose constant support and encouragement
made this book possible

To breast cancer
Thank you for this wake-up call
You have taught me so much

To every woman touched by cancer
You are the inspiration for this book

Thank you

Dearest Sister

If you are reading this now, it's likely that you, or someone close to you is travelling the challenging path of cancer.

It's not a path that anyone would deliberately choose, but having to travel it now for the second time, I'm called to share how I've been navigating it and offer you my companionship on this rocky, yet wondrous road of healing.

I can't know of course, how it is for you, but I do know when this powerful teacher showed up in my life again, so abruptly and shockingly, I wished for the company and guidance of someone who had travelled this path before. I longed for the wisdom of someone who had entered the unknown, dreaded territory and was willing to serve as a guide and companion to my frightened, overwhelmed yet courageous self who was facing this mysterious path and all its powerful gifts.

So, this is that book. It was written for you and the many women around our world whose lives are touched by cancer. It's my hand extended to yours to hold as you navigate your way, to respect you have your own wisest healer within. It's to provide space to uncover what's true for you, to listen to an inner voice that needs to be heard or perhaps to awaken some part of you that's ready to heal and to cherish the life you have now.

On that fateful Friday afternoon when my surgeon confirmed I had breast cancer I was almost paralysed by the force of conflicting, swirling emotions. Anger, frustration, disappointment, denial, grief and devastation. Why me, why now?

Somewhere through all the tears, shock and confusion, once I'd had time to stop, breathe and feel myself, there was a quieter voice rising up in me, calling me to pay attention, to listen and heed the call. I intuitively knew it was time to go within, to meet my pain and transform it. With a second visit from cancer, I chose to meet this unwanted visitor and discover why it was here.

So, I am the wounded healer, sharing my journey even as I travel it.

As I write, I'm in the middle of chemotherapy, deep in my own journey and navigating all manner of insight, pain, confusion, forgotten hurts, beauty and buried treasures. All of it! I have no time to waste as who knows how it's going to turn out but, I want to share with you some of the things that have helped me navigate my treatment with more ease, perspective and tenderness. I am determined to live a rich, meaningful life before, during and after cancer! And I wish this for you too.

I have created this book as the gift I would've liked to receive at the beginning of my soul journey through breast cancer. In sharing my story, I'm validating yours.

I'm here with you, celebrating each step in your unique journey and offering sanctuary, some inspiration and a place to capture your thoughts and feelings, to unearth the treasures of your discoveries and nurture your soul growth.

May this become a gift you pay forward, in time. As each woman's journey is shared, bravely and authentically, it makes an unimaginable difference. To know your suffering has served a purpose and had meaning for another, is a powerful medicine we have almost entirely forgotten. In a culture that values the light, the young, beautiful, functional and healthy, where we deny the inevitability of sickness, aging, death and dying, we are robbed of the rich rewards of travelling to these darker seasons and are collectively the poorer for it.

May you bring your gifts into the light, for yourself, your loved ones and us all.

From my heart to yours.

With so much gratitude,

Cindy Scott xx

"SOMEONE I LOVED ONCE GAVE ME
A BOX FULL OF DARKNESS.

IT TOOK ME YEARS TO UNDERSTAND
THAT THIS TOO,
WAS A GIFT."

Mary Oliver

Contents

Dedication	3
Dearest Sister	4
How to Get the Most From this Book	8
Acknowledgements	9
Understanding and Managing Shock, Fear & Anxiety	10
AUTUMN	**15**
Part 1 : Why me?	16
Part 2 : Prioritising Myself	38
Part 3 : My Circle of Support	68
WINTER	**93**
Part 4 : The Bigger Picture	94
Part 5 : Finding My Power	128
Part 6 : My Body's Wisdom	158
SPRING	**195**
Part 7 : My Inner Sanctuary	196
Part 8 : Trusting My Soul's Plan	222
Part 9 : Accepting What Is	248
SUMMER	**279**
Part 10 : My Wisest Healer	280
Part 11 : Living My Soulful Life	314
Part 12 : Love of My Life	340
Thank You Sister	372
So Much Gratitude	376
References & Recommended Reading	378
My Health Records	380

HOW TO GET THE MOST FROM THIS BOOK

I've written this book more or less as it came to me over these last months. It's been a huge journey in itself and the content isn't necessarily chronological.

The index suggests what is covered in each section, and you may follow the order in which they are presented or feel free to open and dive in wherever you feel drawn, tarot style!

As well as my personal story, each chapter offers inspiration, guidance, self-care practices and rituals. There are resources to follow and plenty of room for you to journal your own experience, using the guided prompts for self-inquiry and insight, if you choose.

Acknowledgements

I wish to thank *Nirado Griffin*, my dear friend and my editor for walking with me every step of the way, masterfully midwifing the birth of this book;

Melissa Williams for artistically designing the book cover to my imagination's desire;

Stephanie Crane for her patience and magic in creating the internal design and layout;

Benay Dyor who despite my reluctance, kept insisting I was a writer;

and most especially *Chris Scott*, my beloved husband, for showing me everyday how to live with love and compassion in my heart.

Finally, I want to thank the *Sunshine Coast* of Australia, for holding me in its beautiful serene surrounds and being the place I most feel at home in the world to write this book.

UNDERSTANDING AND MANAGING
Shock, Fear & Anxiety

I recognise from my own experience, that a diagnosis such as breast cancer invariably comes as a shock.

We are hard-wired for survival, so you may not recognise the symptoms of shock immediately. As your system tries to take in this new information, many neuro-chemical responses are happening at lightning speed in your brain and body and it's likely you'll be functioning in 'survival mode'. This means the more primitive parts of the brain, the brainstem, limbic system and amygdala are activated as the nervous system tries to assess the priorities for your immediate survival. It does however often mean that your higher functioning neo-cortex, where speech, problem solving and complex analysis can go 'offline' as survival takes priority.

Without understanding what's happening physiologically, in an attempt to override the disbelief, or appear 'normal', cope and 'get on with it' you can actually miss important information being shared by your medical practitioners.

Unfortunately, many doctors are not 'trauma-informed' and lack awareness of the impact of a diagnosis as well as treatment on the nervous system.

This is where a friend or ally is so beneficial, as they can support and ground you, take care of your well-being in the moments when you can't and can advocate in your best interests. It is always good to have someone who can accompany you to crucial appointments when needing to take in information and ask questions, particularly about diagnosis and treatment options.

It is a good idea to have some education about the impact of shock on your nervous system as this is likely to come and go throughout your journey.

Everyone responds differently in challenging situations as we have all developed different survival strategies from early childhood, and these are some general guidelines that should be helpful.

Shock is known as the 'freeze' response and indeed, you may feel frozen to the spot, unable to move or take action. There is usually a sudden drop in blood pressure or blood flow throughout the body and you may feel cold, clammy, faint (literally sometimes!) and become dry-mouthed. Your breathing may become shallow, you may hyper-ventilate, feel tingly all over or lose touch with 'reality' and be unable to hear or comprehend what is being spoken.

Whilst it may be a surprise or feel uncomfortable, this is totally normal and part of being in a human body!

Shock can also manifest as a 'flight' response and you feel like running as fast as possible to leave the situation, mobilising all the muscles and narrowing your focus towards 'getting out of here'! Ungrounded, disembodied feelings also result here and if you can be aware enough to stop, breathe, bring yourself 'back into your body', in awareness of the present time and place, it's of benefit to your wellbeing.

Occasionally shock will elicit an unprompted 'fight' response and you can experience the urge to push back, hit out and stop the bearer of bad news. Again, this is an instinctual mechanism of the body trying to protect and defend itself against threat. The breath shortens, skin reddens, muscles may bunch, the fists clench, jaw jutting out in an aggressive stance, ready to fight what's threatening survival.

This response is less common, but is good to know what can occur, so anyone accompanying you knows not to take it personally and with understanding and support can allow this reaction to subside. Tears are very often right under the surface needing to be released and this can help to 'down-regulate' the nervous system to a more tolerable level of experience.

We are often in shock for quite some time after a life-changing diagnosis and you may have a lingering sense of being a bit disconnected, or disassociated, not functioning at your normal level. It comes and goes and you might feel 'just fine' some days and then on others, completely 'out of your body'; light headed, foggy, unfocused, ungrounded, or have a sense of being in a 'parallel universe' where nothing makes sense and you function by rote.

Having compassion for yourself and recognising you deserve care and kindness as you navigate this new territory is the best approach.

There are many practices in this book to help you integrate your experience and allow the body its natural healing processes. There is also more detailed information on the autonomic nervous system in chapter 7 with practises to support the regulation of the sympathetic and parasympathetic branches of the nervous system and increase resilience.

For now, it's good to have some shock 'First Aid' and know how to ground yourself into the present time where you can take the most appropriate choice of action.

Stabilising practices

WHEN IN CRISIS OR UNDER STRESS

Do any of these that feel right in the moment, in no particular order. Practise when you are less activated so you become familiar and can trust your body to know its way to more ease and peace. **Self-resourced. Self love, self care.**

1. **SLOW DOWN.** Take 10 steps very slowly, mindfully, feeling the sensations in your feet and legs, feeling the pull of gravity so you feel solid, heavy and weighted.

2. **Sit on something solid** where you feel safe enough to give over to the sensations of being supported, held or cradled. You can tuck yourself in with a blanket if you are cold or just need to feel swaddled and safe.
Feel the pull of gravity so you feel solid, heavy and weighted, and can feel the sensation where the surface meets your body. See if you can soften and welcome more of that sensation. Notice any places that ease, or release as you follow or track what feels good and pleasurable.
As much as you can, slow your breathing, become curious and bring your focus to the sensations of the body without attaching any 'story' to them.

3. **Slow your breathing** to 5 breaths in, hold for 3, then 7 breaths out. Start with less counts if you can't manage 5 and gradually build up to a steady slow rhythm. Breathe in through your nose, close your eyes if that helps, let the outbreath be gentle and complete easily, holding for a couple of counts before taking the next inbreath. Notice what happens in your body.

4. **Orient.** Ideally sitting somewhere safe, look slowly around, notice the colours and shapes of your surroundings, take in your whole environment with curiosity, letting your gaze rest on something that brings pleasure. Turn slowly to look behind you if you can do so easily, but keep the sensation pleasant. This is literally letting your brain know where you are, that you are safe in this moment and that there are many viewpoints; you have options. Notice what happens in your body.

5. **Connect with your body.** Cross your legs at your ankles, wrap your arms around your body tucking hands under your armpits, lower your head and breathe slowly. Feel the safety and containment of being held. Stay as long as you need to feel calm and more settled.

6.   You can do a version of no 5, above, by wrapping yourself up tight with a blanket, a towel or a sarong. The pressure on the arms particularly lets you know you are safe and able to let breathing and heart-rate return to normal.

7.   **Wrap your arms around you,** as above, instead of tucking your hands into your armpits, let them gently squeeze the muscles of the upper arms, or gently tap from shoulder to elbow. Turn your gaze down or close your eyes, Make it pleasurable and rhythmic, continuing until you feel settled and calm.

8.   **Head Hold.** Put one hand over your forehead and one behind at the base of your neck. Feel the warmth and security of your hands and apply the amount of pressure that feels right. Breathe slowly, notice the sensations in the rest of your body and allow any subtle release, trembling or let go. Sometimes the eyes can flicker and twitch behind the lids, the jaw may unclench and any sighing will indicate the parasympathetic nervous system is engaged.

9.   **Social engagement.** Sometimes the presence of another human can be reassuring, comforting and supportive. If feeling anxious, it can help to just be around people in normal day to day interactions, so any sense of isolation or disconnection can be eased, If you feel the need to share how you are feeling, make sure you have someone you respect and trust to listen compassionately, without giving unsolicited advice and who can maintain confidentiality.

10. **Touch.** Be really attuned to what kind of touch is helpful if at all when you are really anxious, activated or upset. Sometimes just having someone resting hands on your shoulders as you lean back into a chair with eyes closed can be really settling, or gently holding your feet while you breathe to ground yourself. Make sure you stay responsive to what is the right pressure, quality and length of time you receive touch. And sometimes a good long hug from just the right person who can hold you while you wail, or let go is perfect.

11. **Non-human company.** The unconditional loving company of a pet can be a perfect way to settle and regulate yourself when in stress or anxiety. Often dogs, cats, horses and other pets have a very attuned sense for what is needed when their human is upset, so avail yourself of their cuddling and attention if needed.

12. **Hydrate/ Nourish your body.** If ever you've been given bad news, had a medical procedure, or had blood drawn, you may have been offered hot sweet tea and a biscuit in recovery. There is good reason for this, as shock slows the blood flow and you feel cold and numb. Warmth, sugar and hydration can bring you out of the cold of shock, increase circulation and rebalance your blood sugar.

Autumn

PART 1

Why Me?

*"Try not to resist the changes
that come your way.
Instead let life live through you.
And do not worry
that your life is turning upside down.
How do you know that this side
you are used to is better
than the one to come?"*

- Rumi

THANKSGIVING

As I looked around our beautiful dining table complete with crisp white linen tablecloth, flickering candles and crystal glassware, my heart was bursting with so much warmth and joy to be in the company of such an amazing group of people. Thanksgiving is a special time of year for most Canadians and a holiday I love to celebrate. Turkey and pumpkin pie also happen to be some of my favourite foods.

My partner and I had only just moved interstate to the Sunshine Coast in Queensland a few months before but had already met so many wonderful new friends we could invite. As a Canadian living abroad, it feels wonderful to bring some of our customs and traditions to Australia and to offer others an experience of this special time.

As we gathered to share the stunning feast, I took pause and truly gave thanks for that moment, one that will always be imprinted on my heart. You see, I believe we are all powerful manifesters, creators of our reality, so I looked with so much pride at what I had called into my life: a wonderful partner, a move to tropical paradise, a new home, a successful business, beautiful new friends and an abundance of wholesome and delicious food spread before us.

Could life really be any better than this moment?

Following lunch, I asked each of our guests to express something they were thankful for. This is a tradition my mother always insisted on and one I loathed growing up, but now, as the host, I felt inspired to invite everyone to join in this beautiful practise of giving thanks. I was deeply moved by what people shared. I don't think there was a dry eye in the house! So, when the talking stick came around to me, I had so much to be thankful for. In that moment, my life was pretty darn close to perfect.

DISHES

With our bellies full and our hearts even more so, it was time to clean up a mountain of dishes. Some guests had left, others were deep in conversation as Jill and I hovered over the kitchen sink sharing this ordinary moment of domesticity. Despite it being a pretty tedious job, the quieter moments doing dishes together have often led to some of the most profound and intimate conversations I've experienced. We chatted away about my business ambitions and how much I had on my plate. So, when Jill said in her no-nonsense way 'you are such an over-giver, when do you take time to receive from others?', she may as well have spoken in Mandarin. I heard her words but they bounced off me. I was simply not able to comprehend this foreign concept.

TAKE TWO

Just three months later, in a very different setting, I lay there in disbelief as the sonographer, Greg, gently guided his wand over my left breast and said, 'you have a lump'. He said it so quietly I asked him to repeat it. He said it again in a more confident, yet compassionate tone, 'you have a lump'. I fumbled to feel the lump beneath my fingers, my mind racing and vehemently rejecting the notion that breast cancer had returned. It couldn't be. No, not again!

My mind flashed back to my first diagnosis five years earlier. I have already been down this path once before. 'Wasn't that enough?' I silently screamed into the ether, as if someone might hear me or even supply an answer. Inexplicably it seemed, breast cancer was visiting me a second time.

The sonographer handed me some towels to wipe off the gel he used for the ultrasound and I could feel a cold wave of disbelief wash over me. I was like a deer frozen in the headlights as the shock set in. I struggled to form any rational, sensible thoughts at all and stumbled out of the clinic in a blur.

It was like there were two parts of me. My hyperactive, logical mind went into overdrive. In panic, I questioned the prospect of having cancer again and doubted, denied and resisted this reality. I didn't want to believe that cancer had returned. I hadn't even had the biopsy to discover whether it was fatty tissue or in fact a cancerous growth. Maybe they had made a mistake! Meanwhile another part of me, from way deeper down, had already recognised the truth and had determined my diagnosis. I was scrambling to reconcile these opposing voices.

STRIPPED BARE

I had booked to have my annual ultrasound and mammogram just six weeks before our wedding; just another item ticked off my 'to-do' list in the lead up to getting married. With guests flying in from around the world and other parts of Australia, there was absolutely no time for illness, let alone treatment!

However, on that fateful Friday afternoon, my worst fears were realised. As Chris and I sat across from Emma, my breast surgeon, her facial expression communicated her findings before her words did. 'You have cancer', she said. I felt as if someone had knocked the air out of me. I tried to make light of it and put on my brave face but nothing could stop the tears. Words were coming out of her mouth but I don't think I heard anything after the word 'cancer'. Everything inside started reeling as I tried desperately to comprehend what she had said. 'N-n-n-n-o-o-o-o, not again!' went around and around in my head. My body went numb. I went into auto-pilot as we left the clinic.

Outside, nothing had changed; the flowers on the trees shone brightly, the sun beamed in the sky and people went on their merry way. Yet learning the reality of what was happening within me had instantly changed my whole world. I was so grateful to have Chris there to chauffeur me home and take care of me.

With only weeks to go before our wedding date, despite my fear and uncertainty, I went straight into 'handling it'. I had two lots of surgery; one for a lumpectomy and the second, to have a port-a-cath (port) embedded in my chest to make the chemotherapy infusions easier to receive. My oncologist was anxious about leaving my chemotherapy treatments for so long but *nothing* was going to get in the way of our epic, gorgeous, 3-day marriage celebrations.

Life, however, seemed to have other plans, as simultaneously the corona virus was taking centre-stage across the globe. As this unprecedented global pandemic and the rising international panic led to lockdowns and closed borders everywhere, we were forced to cancel our wedding celebrations just two weeks out from the date.

Within the span of just a few short weeks I found myself immersed in a new and frightening world, like a ghastly merry-go-round I couldn't get off. The fear of cancer now gripped me like a vice. I tried to comprehend and digest my diagnosis, was undergoing a barrage of tests and scans, had cancelled our wedding, shut-down my business, commenced chemotherapy and gone into self-isolation with COVID-19. My year was nothing like the one I had envisioned! I felt completely stripped bare of the life I once knew and was in free-fall much of the time, trying to find ground, where there was none.

DETOUR

I didn't need a biopsy to verify what my inner knowing already knew, that I had an aggressive cancer growing inside me. I also knew the bullet-proof mask I normally wear to hide my pain and endure challenges wasn't going to do the trick this time.

I may have skipped lightly through breast cancer the first time around but my second diagnosis was different. The impact was more amplified, intense, the call for action more urgent. In order for me to fully heal, I was going to need to dig a whole lot deeper. Slapping the proverbial band-aid on my situation and believing a lumpectomy would complete my 'healing' wasn't going to cut it. It was merely the first step toward my full body, mind and soul healing.

In our culture, we're taught to avoid painful situations at all cost so my natural reaction to the diagnosis was to avoid, avoid, avoid! My disbelief was palpable and my new reality, my worst nightmare. If there was a detour to bypass this untenable predicament and the painful emotions it evoked, I would've taken it.

I considered the many ways I have successfully numbed and avoided uncomfortable situations in the past. A few too many vinos, some retail therapy, bingeing on the latest Netflix series or keeping myself busy. I'd graduate top of the class for employing creative ways to distract myself and avoid any discomfort!

I am a well-practised pain-avoider, but with this second diagnosis of breast cancer, I knew it was time to take a different path. I also knew it wasn't going to be easy and most likely, it wasn't going to be pleasant, but it's the road I knew I had to take, no matter what I discovered on the way.

THE VOID

When the biopsy confirmed the aggressive cancer growing inside my breast, I felt as if I had been hit by a truck. I was thrust into a new unfamiliar medical world of tests, scans and surgeries and a multitude of unknowns. The door to my old world slammed shut behind me, with no option to return.

Even after the initial shock wore off, I found myself in uncharted territory. Nothing made sense and I had a sense of the ground going out from underneath me.

I call this place the 'void'. Buddhists call it a 'bardo'; the space between. No woman's land.

I think of it like a hallway with a door on either end. I had been shunted into the hallway against my will with one door slammed and padlocked behind me. Until I had a name for it, I ran from this place at all cost. And now I find myself smack dab in the hallway heading towards another door, the door to my future. A door with no obvious key.

No one tells you how long the hallway is, how many turns there are, how bumpy the carpet is or how long it will take to get to the other end. And if you're pain-avoidant like me, making the journey can be a long and arduous one. As I write this book, I am receiving chemotherapy and still very much in the hallway, grieving the loss of what was my life, still often fearful and reluctant to embrace the uncertainty of what lies ahead.

RISING UP

My hallway feels like a rollercoaster at times. There are highs and lows and Eskimo-rolls and parts that scare me to death. I've asked myself a million times, *'What is this all for? What am I here to learn? Why has cancer visited me, again?'* Believe me, there were many days when all I did was curl up on the couch and cry, feeling sorry for myself and creating pity-parties for anyone who'd listen.

Being a first-class victim, however, has never been my style. I have always preferred to be a victor rather than a victim so as I sit in my hallway, contemplating the best way forward, I know this journey is going to be a bumpy and unfamiliar one. However, from a deeper, more tender place inside, I have made a commitment to myself that I am prepared to surrender to any discomfort or vulnerability and trust the process, to allow the insights of this journey to arise.

As I lay in the hospital following my lumpectomy, something radical happened. It seemed as though time stood still. In that moment, any fear I had been feeling was replaced with a sense of calm and a quiet, inner knowing spoke from within. I sensed I had been given a big 'wake-up call' and that in fact, this tumour was a gift. I believe this tumour has something important to teach me.

I knew there would be much more involved to genuinely heal than a quick lick of surgery and to slap a band-aid on my health. To truly heal at a cellular level, I needed to be present to this experience, allowing myself to fully feel my emotions rather than disassociate from them as I so often did. I know this is the key to meeting whatever truth lay buried inside.

In order for some of us to wake up,
we need a wake-up call.

— JOE DISPENZA

THE WAKE-UP CALL

I have always been open to all kinds of healers and am innately curious about the more mystical aspects of life beyond our physical realm. I believe there is a spiritual dimension to life that underlies our everyday experience and connects us all.

I had been having regular treatments with Merryn prior to my diagnosis. She knew me quite well and was already familiar with my physical body when I learned I had cancer. Her treatments were like a lifeline to me, helping me process pain both physically and emotionally. I chose to continue my regular appointments with her as a way of honouring myself and committing to my healing journey.

Merryn is gifted at tuning into the body and has a way of bringing that which is unseen into the light. As I lay on her mat in the chaos of my new reality, crying like a baby, she offered something so profound. *'Your soul will be getting something it wants from all of this'*, she said. And my soul immediately replied with a sigh, *'Yes, I am getting to rest, finally'*.

I have spent much of my life aiming to please others, desperately trying to fit in and not burden others with my needs. In my early life programming, being invisible is much easier than being needy. However, it's also a great way to get overlooked and never receive help.

The truth was, I was exhausted … to the core. Adrenal fatigue wouldn't begin to describe the absolute lethargy I felt. I could barely move. I had nothing left to give.

I was finally able to feel everything I had resisted and repressed for years. I had to acknowledge that desperate feeling that I had to be responsible for it all, could never ask for help, had to keep doing it alone, holding it all together for myself and my son. Desperately trying to keep control of the many fragments that made up my life had finally failed. The cost of those outworn strategies had left me depleted, with no juice left in my tank. I was running on empty.

My breast cancer diagnosis was like hitting a pause button on my life. A wake-up call, waking me up to aspects of my life I was unwilling to see. And at long last, an invitation to rest. Truly, deeply rest.

THE INVITATION

I heard a story once that each of us comes into this life with an essence like a pure and perfect diamond. As we navigate life's challenges, in order to function in the world, we learn to adopt different roles or identities to have our needs met in a variety of ways. These masks, or personalities form subtle layers of protection and armour, slowly building up and gradually, imperceptibly concealing the light of this diamond. Whilst playing these roles can be useful, as we habitually operate through these familiar layers, we start to believe this is who we really are.

The cost however, is this innate brilliance slowly becomes distorted, dulled and buried. Occupied in our daily routines of busyness, relating, care-taking, working and surviving, we may not notice immediately how much of our vital life-force is being drained, diluted and exhausted.

I had a nagging feeling I had lost touch with my true self, I felt like a watered-down version of myself, living a less vibrant life than I knew I was capable of, yet nothing was bad enough or urgent enough to inspire me to change or break out of this habitual, familiar holding pattern.

Until, *THIS!*

Life presented me with a gift – a 'wake-up call' that cracked through my surface armouring, shaking loose those encrusted layers and shining a light on the radiant brilliance buried deep within.

I knew it was time to allow myself to be cracked wide open; to face and feel whatever had been avoided and denied, buried and forgotten for so long.

This journal is my personal story of that radical but necessary rupture. It is a story of heading into the unknown, meeting the fear, the pain, the awkward vulnerability, yet still trusting and following the glimmers of light in the dark. It is about resilience and the capacity of the human spirit to endure and to thrive through adversity. In many ways it's my journey home, my response to my soul's incessant call to recognise the brilliance inside.

As LEONARD COHEN wrote in his beautiful song, ANTHEM:

Ring the bells that still can ring
Forget your perfect offering
There is a crack, a crack in everything
That's how the light gets in.

LOVE IN ACTION

INNER PRACTICE
Just Breathe

Under stress and overwhelm, the flow of oxygen may be impeded, leading to shallow breathing. This means that you are only breathing into your upper chest rather than deep into your belly and thus, into your whole body. Breathing plays a critical role in your health and wellbeing by influencing your parasympathetic nervous system. Deep diaphragmatic breathing communicates to the brain that you are safe and free from harm and thus, initiates a relaxation response.

Let's check your breathing.

Stand in front of the mirror with one hand on your chest and the other on your belly. Take a deep breath. Which hand moved the most? If the hand on your stomach extended reasonably well while the hand on your chest moved minimally, then you are breathing deeply and well. If your chest lifted first with little or no movement in your belly, then your breathing is shallow. That's completely understandable, but choosing to change how you breathe can be remarkably and quickly effective.

Consciously take 10 deep breaths into your belly and feel your body filling out, becoming more 'solid' and awakening a sense of groundedness, or connection to the earth . Practice this throughout the day.

For more ideas refer to the Understanding and Managing Shock section.

OUTER PRACTICE

Being Supported

Who do you have as a support person to take you to appointments and help you make key decisions right now?

What do I most need in this moment? How could I go about having this need met? Is there anything in the way of my asking for this?

How can I support myself in this moment?

How can I be more compassionate towards myself right now?

How can I create more sanctuary in my life to tune into my physical, emotional and spiritual needs?

PART 2

Prioritising Myself

SELFISHNESS

*"I heard a woman on the beach say to her little girl...
"Don't be selfish"
What sad advice.*

*I would give her better.
Be selfish, little girl.
Love yourself well, love yourself first,
then you will love others far, far better*

*Not with grudging show, nor with unfeeling ritual or ... numb duty,
Or self-congratulating sacrifice or stuttering terror of loss*

*Be selfish, little girl
Be best to yourself and rest assured that you will always be...
Joyfully, unstintingly, and if you will give to others, give them most
Help them to be best to themselves too."*

- Stanley M. Herman

SOMEDAY ISLE

If you're like most women, you've been taught to put everyone else's needs first. Isn't that what a 'good' woman should do? Generously giving of yourself to make life easier for others, you make sure your husband, your children, your family, friends and others are cared for as priority. You tell yourself that *'someday isle'* get around to doing things for yourself; one day when everything else is done.

And if you're like me, you get to the end of the day, exhausted and collapse into bed, failing to etch out any time at all for yourself. Day after day, year after year. You justify to yourself that it's okay because you are being of service, selflessly giving to your loved ones and bringing harmony to your world. *'Someday isle'* is more a mirage off in the distance filled with dreams and passions, more like a utopian tropical island than anything that resembles the life you're living.

BREAST CANCER PERSONA

Being of service, nurturing and supporting others to succeed is a wonderful pursuit if it comes from a place of love and abundance. However, many of us continue to give even when we're running on empty. If this way of life becomes habitual, over time it can become the road to resentment, unfulfilled dreams and potentially to ill-health or breast cancer.

In her bestselling book *'The Secret Language of Your Body'*, author Inna Segal unveils the secrets to understanding the messages of our body and reveals the underlying mental, emotional and energetic causes of physical symptoms and specific medical conditions.

Inna suggests there's actually a persona for women who develop breast cancer. She calls it the 'slave' archetype; a woman who feels a lack of nurturing, gentleness and love for herself whilst habitually showering love and compassion onto others.

The
greatest gift
we can give ourselves
is time.

— OPRAH WINFREY

See if any of these persona indicators apply to you, as they did for me!

BREAST CANCER PERSONA

- Never relaxed and calm, always keeping busy doing things
- Tendency to become a workaholic
- Has difficulty saying 'no'
- Desire to please everyone and feeling torn in different directions
- May have feelings of being a victim
- Often overwhelmed and overpowered by others
- Tries to keep everything in control in order not to fall apart
- Difficulty connecting with her own femininity
- Difficulty receiving love, affection and kindness
- Feeling like she doesn't need help from others, she can take care of herself
- Overburdening herself with responsibilities
- Not having any clear boundaries
- Always worrying about everyone and everything
- Deep need to be liked and please others

On that morning when my surgeon shared the news of my diagnosis, I was conflicted. I recalled my first encounter with breast cancer, just five years earlier and was reminded of how I responded to its appearance back then.

I was a single Mom then and chose to traverse my journey alone. I shared my diagnosis with only a select few close friends, I continued to 'soldier' on with my work and retreated from the world socially as I went through my treatment feeling separate and alone.

I wore my bullet-proof armour, put my big-girl pants on and decided I could handle this myself. I never really let people know what I was going through, in some way denying that my diagnosis was actually real. I refused to accept there was anything 'wrong' with me and would not take any time to acknowledge what was taking place in my body nor give myself any time to rest and heal. I was just too busy. I had a business to run and bills to pay. Following my lumpectomy, I really couldn't be bothered with radiation and taking time to rest, so I refused further treatment entirely.

Without realising it, I had been a classic 'slave' for much of my life. Trying to fit in, trying to make life easier for my husband, to placate him when he became my ex-husband, to run my business and make sure I had enough money to raise my son as a single Mom. My life has always been busy and full so the notion of taking time out for me has always been a luxury. It actually felt too self-indulgent and not something I could justify for myself.

DENIAL

When confronted with a second diagnosis of breast cancer, my immediate reaction was the same as the first time around; sweep it under the carpet and it will go away. I told myself, just have the lumpectomy and get on with things. You haven't got time for this. You have a business to run, a wedding to organise, a son to put through university. There is absolutely no time or space in your life for this insidious, unwelcome visitor.

However, when my biopsy results showed I had an aggressive cancer growing in my breast as well as in my lymph nodes, I knew I really needed to pay attention. This time, I had to do things differently. I may have escaped it the first time around, but my inner knowing advised I wouldn't be able to pull it off a second time.

So, when my friend Stacy shared the potential emotional and energetic causes of breast cancer in Inna Segal's book, I intuitively knew there was a gift in this for me that was worth exploring.

Your own self-realisation
is the greatest service
you can render the world.

- RAMANA MAHARSHI

THE DILEMMA

A cancer diagnosis is like hitting the pause button on your life. Whether you are ready for it or not, the universe is insisting you stop and focus on yourself. There is little alternative.

As I weighed up all the elements of my life and determined what would need to go, my business was the hardest. I am like many women who love the sense of purpose and achievement I get from it. Would I be able to continue working throughout my treatment? Would I have the energy and focus that my work demanded? At the same time, would I be giving myself the appropriate time to rest and repair if I continued working?

I was conflicted. The egoic part of me wanted desperately to put on a brave face and continue working, be strong and 'soldier on', while the quieter voice within me was saying, 'just stop', give up the struggle.

I sat with my plight for several days and consulted some of the sage elders I am blessed to call friends. When you're in the midst of chaos, I find getting an objective, unemotional perspective invaluable. After sharing my situation, my dear friend Vida asked me the golden question, 'What would you advise another woman to do in your situation?'.

And in that moment, I knew I would never advise another woman to push through her diagnosis and treatment, choosing her career over giving herself the much-needed time to rest and heal. So why was I not prepared to give that to myself?

It was time to get real with others and more importantly, with myself. To be honest and v-v-v-vulnerable. Oh God, that's something I don't know how to do! I have no idea how to let others see my soft underbelly, to acknowledge that I am not okay and that I actually need help.

HEALTHY BOUNDARIES

One of the most profound ways we take care of ourselves is through setting loving boundaries. Boundaries can be emotional, psychological, energetic or physical. In a very real way, a healthy felt sense of our boundaries lets us know the extent of what is 'me' and what is not. Our boundaries protect what is most important to us. They help us to acknowledge where we have control within our domain and show us how to respect the boundaries of others.

I needed to re-evaluate the boundaries that defined my life. *Were they working for me? Did they need re-defining? Did I need to create new ones to ensure I protected myself in the coming months?*

The best time to relax is when you don't have time.

— CHINESE PROVERB

BEING SEEN

With my heart in my throat, I reluctantly began to write an email to my customer base. If I was going to be the type of leader I would admire, I needed to accept my diagnosis as the seismic thunderbolt it was and come clean with my clients, but more importantly with myself. I would demonstrate this by establishing a healthy loving boundary for myself and my business.

Writing that email was one of the hardest things I've had to do. I wrote a heart-felt letter informing them of my diagnosis, letting them know that I would be closing my business indefinitely to give myself the space and time I needed to seek treatment, to rest and fully heal. This was a massive, courageous, painful step for me to put myself first and make my treatment a priority. How crazy is that?

I was so worried what people would think. I assumed that my customers and business collaborators would be upset with me. I felt I had let them down and they would be disappointed in me. With dread in my heart, I hit send.

The response was amazing. In just minutes, I was overwhelmed by an outpouring of love, understanding and generosity. My thoughts of being a burden and disappointing others, was met with so much support. I felt seen, heard and loved because I was willing to share my truth. And a small crack began to show in my stoic, polished veneer.

Where had I learned to put everyone else's needs before my own, to shower love and support on others and not give any to myself, first? Even with such a loud call to pay attention to my body, I struggled to give myself permission to be a priority in my own life. It felt like a well-worn path of martyrdom that kept me on a slow boil of resentment and it was beginning to bubble over. Boy, did I have some work to do!

STOP SHOULD-ING

One of my favourite authors and greatest teachers is Louise Hay. In her wonderful book *'Heal Your Life'*, Louise challenges us to consider where the 'shoulds' are in our life. Are you living from a place of 'you should do this or that' or from a place of inspiration, love and joy?

As the eldest child, I felt a strong sense of responsibility to be a 'good' girl and do the 'right' things. Without ever questioning it, my life had become a long list of *'shoulds'*. *'You should do this'*, and *'don't do that'*, I could hear my parents' well-intentioned voices in my head, guiding me. They wanted me to be the best person I could be and to be a role model for my sisters.

I did the best I could, but what I realised is that living from a place of *'should'* and to please others expectations, rather than inspiration, is a sure-fire way to suck any joy and happiness out of any activity, even when it's something you love to do.

I decided it was time to stop 'should-ing' myself and instead, choose joy. I started paying attention to *why* I was doing what I was doing, noticing whether my actions were motivated from a place of love and joy or was I acting out of duty? Like loosening the rigid gates of a lock, I gradually began to allow the stream of joy to flow through me with greater ease.

LOVE IN ACTION

INNER PRACTICE

Being in the Present

Fostering a quiet connection with yourself is one of the most important ways to calm an overwhelmed nervous system, reduce stress and bring you back into a balanced state. Even in all the busy-ness of it's possible to find small chunks of time for yourself and practice meditation to cultivate an inner life.

Meditation offers great health benefits as it activates the parasympathetic nervous system, decreases cortisol, reduces respiration and heart rate. The increased blood flow to the brain oxygenates the cells and allows a greater state of relaxation.

As I have a hyper-active monkey mind, I prefer a guided meditation that gently gives my monkey something to do so I can more easily find the quiet within. I have created a number of guided meditations just for you… can I suggest starting with the Breathing Meditation which you can find on my website.

OUTER PRACTICE

My Healing Sanctuary

Create a lovely space in your home that is your healing space. Find items that you love like candles, fresh flowers, essential oils, diffuser, Healing Journal, favourite pens, a soft blanket; anything that makes it feel as though it is your sanctuary, and it is sacred.

Claim this space as your special place to honour yourself and practice many of the techniques throughout this book. Dedicating a space as your sanctuary can literally gather and hold the cumulative energy of all your intentions. This creates a strong anchor so that every time you enter this space it becomes easier and easier to find your centre.

just breathe

If my best friend was in this situation, what advice would I give her?

What would I need to let go of so I could put myself and my healing journey first, without guilt or apology?

What feelings or emotions come up for me when I consider putting myself first?

What do I habitually do when those feelings come up?
How else could I meet those feelings with more compassion?

Am I willing to fiercely love and accept myself through my healing journey?

Where do I run over myself and go faster than I need to?

Where do I have boundaries in my life that are working for me?

Where do I need new boundaries to honour what's sacred to me?

If there were no rules or expectations, I would ...

Calm

PART 3

My Circle of Support

"Sometimes our light goes out, but is blown again into instant flame by an encounter with another human being."

- Albert Schweitzer

LESSON LEARNED

When I was first diagnosed with breast cancer five years ago, in what I affectionately call my 'test' run, I wanted to hide away from everyone. I was ashamed of my diagnosis. I didn't think people would understand me or what I was going through. I started to isolate myself from friends and family even though care and compassion was the thing I needed most. I felt separate and alone.

I shared my struggle with just a couple of close friends. I didn't want to tell my wider friendship circle and work colleagues as I have never been comfortable with being vulnerable. Vulnerability has always been synonymous with weakness for me and being weak is the last thing I would ever want to be! That, and being dependent, needy or a burden. Ugh!

I chose instead to shoulder the burden alone. Separating myself from the love and support of others and in my own way, refusing to acknowledge that there was actually something wrong with me.

I didn't have time to stop working and attending to the many responsibilities that made up my life and I wasn't prepared to carve out any time for treatment and rest. It was non-negotiable for me to stop. Instead, I faced my diagnosis like any other speed bump in my life and attempted to solve it like a problem that could be handled with my usual pragmatic efficiency.

On a subconscious level, what I was saying was that I was simply not important enough to take the time to invest in my health and wellbeing. If I had a flat tire or my car needed an oil change, I would book it in for servicing immediately, but somehow the care and maintenance of my bodily vehicle was different. How crazy is that?

So, when I received my second diagnosis, every cell in my body wanted to shrink away from this reality and separate myself from loved ones, to do this on my own, yet again. Somehow the shame of yet another diagnosis felt magnified as I now had even more at stake than five years ago. I had a business to run, bills to pay and a shiny veneer to uphold. Or so I thought.

This time however, I had a loving and supportive husband, Chris. Yes, this amazing man chose to follow through and marry me following my diagnosis! We cancelled our elaborate wedding plans and instead, opted for an intimate, covid compliant ceremony with just a celebrant and two witnesses.

Chris refused to buy into my defiant, 'she'll-be-right' nature and instead of letting me sweep my diagnosis under the carpet, he encouraged me to be vulnerable and to share my journey with our loved ones. In his mind, our family and friends deserved to know and would want to support me through this.

This willingness to be vulnerable with others has been the single most potent difference between my first journey and this one. To risk the exposure and discover that I am loved, appreciated and worthy of compassion has been one of the toughest yet most beautiful gifts I've received from having breast cancer.

I am continually surprised how caring and compassionate people are, sometimes from those you least expect(!), and how they love to give their support when we are vulnerable enough to let them in. I feel so much gratitude for the many people that make up my circle of support. Learning to receive loving kindness has been a humbling lesson, but one that has been so nourishing for my soul.

HUSBANDS

The first several months of treatment were much more introspective than I had anticipated and my focus was on how I was feeling, learning how to manage the side effects of chemotherapy and all the accompanying physical changes. I had very little capacity or energy to support the needs or feelings of others during this time, including my beloved husband, Chris.

My diagnosis sent a shock wave through our brand-new marriage and shifted the dynamic of our relationship significantly. It was all about me and my needs and by default, Chris became my primary carer. I was on an emotional rollercoaster coming to terms with who I was now, as the labels I had used to define myself - business woman, go-getter and social butterfly fell away along with my hair. I didn't think losing my hair was going to be that big of a deal but, when it started falling out in clumps I was horrified. Just weeks after our gorgeous, intimate wedding day where my hair looked stunning, all that was left now were a few straggly clumps here and there; a daily reminder that I am in treatment for cancer.

Chris, who has a big, generous heart and desire to make life easier for me in a multitude of ways, stood by feeling powerless as I slowly fell apart, knowing that all he could do was watch. As much as he would have liked to 'fix' me and this situation, it was pretty unfixable.

Ask for what you want
and be prepared to get it.

- MAYA ANGELOU

I have always been a high-achieving, independent woman but as I moved into chemo treatment, I was nauseous and unwell and became increasingly reliant on my husband to manage our domestic duties, meal preparation and chauffeuring me to my myriad appointments. Almost overnight, I had shifted from being self-reliant to becoming heavily dependent on Chris financially, emotionally and socially. He became my link to the outside world, the keeper of my emotional wellbeing and the practical decision maker in times when my mind had gone to mush.

I will be forever grateful to Chris for being my rock and absolute support through all of this. In saying that, I believe supporting a woman through breast cancer is a massive undertaking and is the work of many people, like in a village. It is just too much for one person to hold, no matter how deep and close the relationship.

Chris was keeping himself together and staying strong for my benefit, but his life had also been turned upside down. As he was adapting to the radical changes in me, he had his own inner world of turmoil, was being stretched to his capacity and had very little emotional support from me. As much as my intimate partner played a significant role in my life and healing journey, he was also going through his own journey, navigating his way through the labyrinth and deserving of good support and comfort.

I underestimated the absolute importance of friendships during this time, and will be forever grateful for every single phone call, conversation, card, gift and hug that helped lift my spirits and affirm that I am loved throughout the most challenging time of my life.

THE LONG HAUL

I have always had a propensity to make things happen and get things done; a no-nonsense independent girl with a strong desire for results. I love ticking things off my to-do list and the sense of achievement upon completing things.

Unfortunately, cancer treatment is not the type of journey you can skip through quickly and tick off your list. It's much more of a marathon than a sprint. Not a flat, gentle marathon but a bumpy, up-hill exhausting climb at times. It's also not a solo race but one which requires the support of others. In fact, it would be nearly impossible to do this alone.

'They say it takes a village to raise a child. I believe it takes a community to help heal from cancer.'

A friend
is someone who knows the
song of your soul
and sings it back to you
when you've forgotten the words.

- ANONYMOUS

Going through treatment has been one of the toughest journeys of my life. When I reflect on the people who supported me most, it was those who had the capacity to sit with my distress and intense emotions, to see me at rock bottom, in the rubble and unconditionally hold space for me there. I didn't need to be 'fixed' in this situation but rather needed someone who could allow what was coming up for me, whether it made sense or not, without judgment.

One of the greatest challenges for me throughout my treatment was shifting from a 'doing' focus to one of 'being' or stillness. Coming from a world that's fast-paced, results driven and keeping busy is a badge of honour, the notion of stillness was completely foreign and had no value. I had no idea what it meant to stop, to truly rest, to be still, nor did I have any strategies on how to 'do' stillness. I wanted to jump-start my treatment plan and get to the other side of it, ASAP!

Much to my horror, I found there was no fast-track or short-cut to get me 'through it all' quickly. It's a long, long road and one that requires real staying power, not only for the one in treatment, but also for the people that make up the circle of support.

THE UNEXPECTED

I consider myself pretty fortunate to have many wonderful and generous people in my life. People who show their care and compassion for me every day and even more so when I'm going through tough times. My circle of support is vast and varied. Many people truly showed up to support me through my treatment in ways I could never have imagined.

What I didn't expect was the way some people, those close ones I had assumed would be there, did NOT show up for me, at all! I spent many nights tossing and turning in hurt and anger and disbelief. My life had literally flipped upside down with a diagnosis that had rocked me to the core and caused sudden and drastic changes to my world. And they never called. They didn't ask how I was going. Nothing. Their silence was deafening!

I felt so alone. So hurt, so rejected, and so deeply ashamed.

I couldn't be hurt any deeper than this. To feel abandoned in the hour of most need cuts straight to my deepest, oldest wound. Abandonment. THIS is the wound that festers for me. Deep, untended and unhealed. Unworthiness.

My inner child raged and railed at them all.

'How could people be so cold? So heartless? So utterly lacking in compassion?'

'When I'm completely devastated, they look the other way.'

'Do they not love me? Don't I matter to them?'

How do I reconcile that? They are either too busy to care or they actually just don't care. I'm not sure which is worse.

My old defence strategy is to walk away. Shut them out, pretend it doesn't matter. Bury the hurt right back down again. I could feel the walls of my Fort Knox growing thicker and taller. I hit some pretty dark places wondering why they didn't care enough to reach out. So much so, I started working with a psychologist, Keely, who helped me to find a new perspective and make peace with behaviours I couldn't understand.

I came to realise that whilst my diagnosis may have been a shock to me, its impact is felt by others in ways only they will ever know. It is especially true for the friends and family who are closest to us, that the ripple effect can be most strongly felt. Considering that their behaviour said more about their capacity to handle my situation, and the radical changes to our usual ways of relating was unfamiliar. I am so used to making other's behaviour mean something about me and that it must be my fault. I've failed to please them. We can never fully comprehend how others perceive us and relate to what we're going through. People are not obliged to make me feel better. My happiness is my responsibility. I may have less emotional charge and more perspective now, but these personal dynamics are something I continue to work with.

ANSWERS

For many weeks, I was filled with so much anger and hurt. I was exhausted and spiralling deeper into this quagmire. I rang my friend Benay to give me some comfort and help find strategies to make peace with the challenges I was having with this absence of contact from friends and family. Benay and I share a love of Australia and are both thousands of miles from our birthplace, so I knew she would be the perfect friend to shed some light on my situation. After relaying my version of the story to her, she asked one simple question, *"And where are you not giving the love, attention and care you seek to yourself?".*

Wham, right between the eyes! Of course, this isn't actually about *them* and what they're doing to *me*, it is a projection of what I am experiencing *within me*.

Even though it still felt true that some people did a crap-ass job of keeping in touch, or showing any sign of regard or compassion for my situation, I realised that I would be much better focused on how I could initiate and embody loving ways to help sustain and nourish my soul, rather than suffer in waiting or expecting others to do so.

Message received loud and clear!

There are only two ways to live your life.
One is as though nothing is a miracle.
The other is as though everything is a miracle.

- ALBERT EINSTEIN

SUPPORT TEAM

Working with Keely the psychologist helped me see that different people bring different specialities to the table. Some may offer care, compassion, comic relief, advice, meaning-making, be a sounding board or distraction and so on.

I came to a place in my healing where I began to marvel at those who reached out, and felt how they lifted my spirits with their kindness. I had gratitude for every contact I received, knowing that I was being held by people who cared enough to get in touch. I realised that every person is caring and contributing to my journey in ways only they can.

It is so hard for me to be vulnerable, to share my feelings, to open myself and truly be seen, but I must. I can't do this alone. I do need help and support and I need the love others are so willing to give.

Letting go of my need to 'manage' that which was happening around me, relaxing into being held and supported by others and surrendering to powers greater than me were key to my healing. I could no longer uphold the superwoman persona I wore so well. I didn't have the energy nor the inclination. She washed away as well. I'm not sure if it was out of conscious choice or my sheer exhaustion but releasing my grip on the reins of my life and allowing the assistance of others was all I could muster. Relaxing into the loving support of others has been such a beautiful experience for me.

LOVE IN ACTION

INNER PRACTICE
Calling in Support

Go to a space that is sacred to you. It might be the space at home you have dedicated as your sanctuary. Centre yourself with some breaths and feel the weight of your body settle into the surface you're sitting on. Feel that as support.

Close your eyes and gently lean back into your chair, expanding your chest, opening your heart and tuning in to the subtle sensations of your precious living body.

Feel where you are currently supported in all forms. This includes people, ancestors, guides, pets, resources, your home, places in nature.

Visualise your circle of support. Even if you don't have physical access to all of them right now, imagine that circle gathering around you and feel yourself being nourished and supported by them. Be curious at the different ways this support can arrive!

Notice what shows up when you do this practice.

OUTER PRACTICE
Asking for Support

Who are the people I feel most supported and uplifted by? In whose company do I naturally feel I'm able to be my natural self?

_____

_____

_____

_____

Is there anywhere I resist asking for and receiving support?

Who do I choose to have in my circle of support? List them here.

How could I lovingly allow others to support me?
Do I have any resistance to receiving that support, no matter how subtle?

Who are the people I most lean on in tough times? Can I count on them now?

How would it feel to be fully held and supported on my journey?

How could I give myself the love and care that I need when others aren't available?

Relax

Winter

PART 4

The Bigger Picture

*Nothing binds you except your thoughts;
Nothing limits you except your fears;
And nothing controls you except your beliefs.*

- Marianne Williamson

NAPALM

The day arrived for my first chemo infusion. I had already taken a tour of the clinic to familiarise myself with the venue and staff, but nothing could have prepared me for this confronting appointment. The lump of plastic, the port in my chest where they would inject the chemo drugs was already giving me grief. I found it hard to ignore the irritating presence of this foreign object under my skin.

I waited half an hour for them to call me in, getting increasingly anxious and having a hard time staying present. All my grounding practices went out the window and I couldn't do a thing to calm my jittery nerves. I felt like I was on death row waiting for the electric chair.

As if it wasn't already scary enough, when I was in the treatment room, the nurse approached wearing a full protective gown and gloves to keep him safe from the poison he was about to administer. My heart rate was peaking!

He struggled to find my port, trying over and over to stick the needle into the port. I have never liked needles and can't bear the sight of them, so I sat rigid in absolute horror as he tried repeatedly to find it. Twenty-five minutes later, feeling like a pin-cushion with my anxiety now through the roof, he finally called over another nurse who managed to find my port on the first go. Thank heavens!

Well, my body rarely takes medicine or supplements of any sort; and it revolted. I felt fine as Chris drove me home. I had a cup of tea and thought I was managing just fine … and then the wheels fell off. The nausea set in, my stomach churned and all I could think about was vomiting this disgusting feeling away. I felt like I'd been poisoned and my body was trying to get rid of it. I tried to throw up, but nothing would come. It was awful and debilitating and continued for the whole following week.

CONFLICTED

As I sat in the reception area waiting for my second round of chemo treatment, I felt a familiar wave of anxiety coursing through me, as I do at every visit. I've not known anxiety too often in my life and I haven't developed many coping strategies for it. I prefer to live my life a little more relaxed and free-flowing! Yet undergoing chemo treatment has stirred up all sorts of uncomfortable emotions and most dreaded is the pervasive and paralysing anxiety. It's like this under-lying anxiety is my constant companion now, colouring every waking hour with its shallow breath, clammy palms and quickened heart rate.

I had a session with my healer friend Merryn yesterday. I love to go see her not only for the physical bodywork she does with me, but for the profound conversations she initiates and the pearls of wisdom she shares.

She asked me if I was conflicted about my treatment plan. She said, *"it seems a part of you is accepting that chemo is part of your healing journey, whilst there's another part kicking and screaming that pouring toxic chemicals into your body feels wrong and CAN'T be your pathway to health!"*.

She was absolutely right. I appeared to be willingly receiving chemo infusions in the hope of killing off the cancer cells, whilst another part of me was vehemently REJECTING these toxic drugs being injected into my veins. After billions of dollars have been raised and spent on researching this insidious disease, I cannot believe that THIS is the best, most effective treatment the medical fraternity can come up with! It just doesn't feel like the best way to optimal health.

ANXIETY PRESENTS

After four napalm-quality chemo infusions, my oncologist was changing my cocktail of drugs. That's what his medical training has taught him to prescribe for someone with my particular diagnosis.

The first four treatments were extremely hard on my body. I felt horribly sick for the week following chemo and then I'd mostly recover in the second week, just in time for my next treatment and so the cycle continued. So, the thought of commencing a new drug for another twelve treatments conjured up more fear and dread, as I didn't know how I would handle it.

As I sat in the reception area, waiting to be called in for the first of my twelve new chemo treatments, I could feel my anxiety building. It had been building for days and I could feel it in my body. My tummy was doing flip-flops and I wanted to throw up. I felt stressed, tired and resistant to my pending treatment.

I sat in the chemo clinic, churning inside. Afraid, bewildered yet mostly defiant. It was like a tug of war being fought by different parts within me and the tension in my body was unbearable.

One part was saying I do NOT want this shit in my body and it is NOT OK to be submitting to this! She was angry, frustrated and resistant. She felt trapped without options and felt powerless in the face of the 'medical system.'

We are what we think.
All that we are arises with our thoughts.
With our thoughts, we make the world.

— BUDDHA

The other part was saying 'I am so scared of what lies ahead and what might happen if I don't take this treatment. I'm not ready to die. I'm sooooo not ready to die!' So, in the end, both parts reluctantly submit to the process.

Christine, the most amazing and compassionate nurse at the clinic is taking care of me on this day. She is my favourite of all the staff. Sadly, this is her second last day at work as she heads off on maternity leave to have her first child. I am disappointed she won't be there to take care of me in the months ahead.

She told me about all the side effects I may experience throughout this treatment as well as those I may experience at the onset of receiving the infusion. Suddenly, it was all too much for my super-stressed and overwrought nervous system. It was like the floodgates opened and all the stoicism and the brittle polish of my veneer could no longer withstand the pressure welling up inside. I burst into uncontrollable tears like a two-year old. Rivers of tears streamed down my face. I could no longer contain the pent-up anger, fear and anxiety that needed to be released.

Christine was so amazing and just encouraged me to let the tears fall. She sat with me and held space for me as it all emptied out. *Isn't this what crying is for?*

CAGED LIONESS

I felt trapped like an animal imprisoned in a cage at the zoo. Uncertain, out of control, my freedom taken and my environment controlled. I'm habitually impatient, so the thought of another whole year of treatment, surgeries and more drugs felt like hiking up a mountain I just didn't want to climb. I am only just starting on this fucking journey and I don't want any of it. I'm burning with rage that THIS is the best that the medical fraternity can come up with??!!

Yet here I am, travelling down this road … one I don't want to be on. Following my doctor's orders obediently when every cell in my body says 'hell no'. Why me? Why has cancer visited me again? Why do I have to go through this?

I just want to quit. I want to go back to my life as it was. However, even if I wanted to give up and try to go back, I know I can't. The door behind me is firmly closed. We are amidst the COVID pandemic and life will never be the same. There is no looking back. We are heading toward a 'new' normal, whatever that means.

Am I sad? Am I grieving the loss of what was? You bet I am!

I can get myself excited about a new future beyond all this but there is something gritty and ugly that I need to face here first and I can't quite put my finger on it. It's deep, it's primal, it's dark. I haven't been here before, ever. What are you trying to tell me? What do I need to see that I haven't been willing to see until now?

EGOIC DEATH

My good friend, Bart suggests that part of my ego is dying, that I am literally dying to something, and that my soul is having an upgrade. I like the sound of that; an upgrade. It's a nice way to put it.

What egoic part of myself am I dying to? What do I need to let go of?

Everything my identity has been built on has been eroded; my career, my looks, my health, my body, my lifestyle, my relationships, my freedom. Every single fucking last thing! It's like being in quicksand where the ground was firm before.

My career … well, I hadn't been happy with it for a long time. I'd been pushing for change but not really finding inspiration and alignment there.

My looks … well, I have never got to the stage of looking in the mirror and loving what I see there. My inner critic always has something derogatory to say, about my hips, my breasts, my nose.

My health… well, my fitness has gone out the window. I don't feel like doing any exercise, but then I never really enjoyed doing exercise. It's always been a 'should' I endured with little enjoyment for an elusive outcome. I notice my body getting flabbier and my cardio fitness is completely gone.

My relationships … if there's anything that helps bring clarity to who is really genuinely supportive of you no matter what, breast cancer will do it. The friends and family that do care show their support, while others just disappear. Whatever their experience, it bloody well hurts when people I expected would be there for me, just aren't. It's VERY hard to refrain from burning bridges and casting those relationships aside for good. It's so hard to find compassion in it all, and some days, it still makes me mad as hell and cuts me to the core.

My freedom … this is the one that sucks the most. So much that I've taken for granted in my life is now gone. The freedom to travel, mingle with people, shop freely, eat and drink without concern, walk without being out of breath, have sex without fear. I don't like to be told no, to be denied, to be trapped or feel at the mercy of anyone else. And that's exactly where I am.

RESISTANCE

What we resist, persists.

I have enjoyed good health most of my life. I eat well most of the time, live in a place that nourishes my soul and have a loving partnership with my husband. The news of my second diagnosis just floored me. I have had a hard time reconciling that cancer has found me once again. After all the good work I have done and the personal development I have been committed to for many years, *have I not done enough work, have I not got enough lessons? What more do I need to do?*

My parents are salt-of-the-earth-people who cultivated many of the values I cherish in my life. One of those is my determination to face whatever life's challenges come my way with a spirit of 'life is precious and I'm prepared to do what it takes to survive.' They may not have done this intentionally, but they instilled a belief that the body has intelligence to restore its own balance, that doctors are educators and medicine is to be taken sparingly.

I have a strong aversion to medications and rarely fulfil the many prescriptions I have been given over the years. I prefer to believe that I am my own best healer.

So, receiving my diagnosis and being given a treatment plan of chemotherapy, a bevy of anti-nausea medications, a double mastectomy, full hysterectomy and tamoxifen has been a very hard pill to swallow, pardon the pun. I have HUGE resistance to my path ahead. I don't want this cocktail of drugs in my body. I don't want to lose my breasts and reproductive organs. And I don't want to take more and more pills, for years to come.

Can you see my dilemma? I want and demand to be my own healer but somehow, this all feels much bigger than me. Having a team of medical specialists with their years and years of study and experience advising me on my treatment plan and I don't want any of it!

I don't think I am in denial about having breast cancer, I just really struggle to believe that pouring a cytotoxic cocktail into my veins, that will burn my skin on contact or wreak havoc on my septic system, is the right most peaceful solution to bringing my body back into balance.

I have so much resistance to this treatment path and I am positive that in fifty years' time, this approach will be deemed barbaric and unimaginable. For now, however, this is the best that modern medicine has come up with and it is my fate.

I have been meditating every day to try to settle my fears and find calm. I need to find a way to surrender to and make peace with it; to find a way to accept it into my body, believing with every cell of my being that this treatment plan is the correct path towards restoring my body, mind and soul.

WHAT THE ...?

I met a wonderful lady named Gail on one of my first visits to the clinic. It is amazing how life weaves its magic and new friends appear even in the darkest of times. Gail is a 'joy-germ', someone who spreads joy and laughter wherever she goes. Whenever she came into our chemo clinic, she wore a big, contagious smile and brightened the day for everyone around her.

As I got to know Gail throughout our treatments together, we compared our experiences and discussed the side-effects. Despite having the exact same treatment regime, we were having an entirely different experience. Gail was literally bouncing through her napalm infusions, continuing to live a full life and even enjoying a few vinos along the way. Her side effects were minimal.

What was I doing wrong? I felt nauseous, lethargic, lousy. My favourite foods no longer tasted good and my one vice, a nice chilled sauvignon blanc was undrinkable, the taste now completely unpalatable. What the ...? How was Gail having such a positive and seemingly easy journey, when mine was a living hell?

I asked myself how this might be possible. I am a professional leadership coach and have a large toolkit of resources at my disposal, but it hadn't dawned on me until that moment how powerful our thoughts can be; powerful enough to shape the meaning and therefore, the experience of an event.

The meaning Gail was giving to her treatment plan was a pragmatic, emotionally neutral one. She was happy to receive her infusions and saw this as her pathway to optimal health. The story I was writing was quite different.

THE STORY

I found myself using words like 'I'm battling cancer', 'I'm climbing a mountain I don't want to climb', 'It's a crap shoot', 'I'm enduring my treatment' and 'I'm having another napalm infusion'. My words felt dense and negative and made me feel that way too.

How could I reframe these descriptors to still acknowledge what I'm going through, but in language that is gentler and more loving? As I considered the 'story' Gail was telling herself about her experience, I was reminded just how important our attitudes are and how powerful the impact of the language we use.

How we see anything,
changes everything.

– MEGGAN WATTERSON

What is the story I'm telling myself? As the author of my story, what could I write that would be more nurturing and supportive to my healing and growth?

Between the *stimulus & response* there is a space, and in that space is your *power* and your *freedom.*

- VIKTOR FRANKL

THREE DOORS

It occurred to me there are three distinct doors, or perspectives I could choose to view my treatment path.

1 The Victim

Victims take the extreme view that the treatment is poison, it will burn or harm, they will suffer and it's not the best pathway to health. Victims meet treatment with defiance and refusal, as though they are powerless and they are being subjected to it against their will. This is where the patient feels she has no control and her life must be put on hold while enduring treatment, with an uncertain outcome. It can feel quite traumatic and more like a prison-sentence.

2 In Gratitude

The other end of the spectrum are women who take the view that chemo and radiation is actively killing their cancer cells and is a necessary part of their healing process. As they maintain a positive outlook that their treatment is helping them, they have little resistance and welcome any treatment into their body with ease and acceptance. They believe they can continue to live a full life throughout their cancer treatment and have a high level of optimism that their life will get back to normal. There is a sense this route is a choice they are empowered to make and thus, is far less traumatic.

3 The Middle Way

In many ways, women in this space feel neutral about their treatment and simply accept it is the best option. There is little angst or resistance here but rather, a more pragmatic approach to treatment.

SHIFTING FOCUS

I am actually embarrassed to admit that I was definitely in the 'victim' doorway and all of my coach training had flown out the window. Until I had the beautiful reminder brought by Gail's absolute grace and serenity throughout her treatment, I had no concept that there was another way to travel through this.

During the first couple of months, I had almost constant nausea and continually wanted to vomit. My stomach was doing flip-flops, I felt horrible and angry at the world that I had to go through this.

I started to connect the dots … *what if the state of my stomach was somehow related to the state of my mind? Could they be related?* Of course! The body and mind are inextricably linked and we cannot affect one without the other.

My inner sceptic would never let me fully make the jump through the 'Grateful' door, but I knew intuitively that the 'Middle' door was probably a much healthier place for me if I was going to endure the long road ahead without creating unnecessary suffering.

NEVER TRUST

I heard a woman at a mindfulness conference once say, 'Never trust your thoughts'. At first this was shocking for me to consider. *What do you mean? Aren't my thoughts what's really going on for me?* It's who I truly am. Shouldn't I trust them? And the answer is no …

Have you ever had the experience of recounting a past event with a sibling or friend? I recall the time my son and I went to a theme park and went on the roller-coaster together. One of us found the experience exhilarating and the other was terrified! How can it be that two people experience the same event and have very different memories of it?

It is to do with our thoughts. What did you think about the event? What were you feeling in the moment and what meaning did you assign it? Thoughts arise, fed by impressions and sensations yet the meanings we attach to them become habitual and unquestioned. Yes, we are the authors creating our story each day, and we have CHOICE. Having this knowledge has TOTALLY changed my life.

I began to practise detaching from my thoughts and getting really curious about them. *Where did they come from? Why was I thinking what I was thinking? Was there another way of thinking about this right now?* I started creating space around my thoughts.

For my own sanity, I needed to challenge unhelpful thoughts that prevented me embracing my journey with ease and grace. This is a bit like building a muscle, it takes practice, the more practice the better.

A thought that arose time and again during my treatment was the sheer paradox of my experience. On the one hand, it was one of the most terrifying, traumatic experiences I've endured and at the same time, one of the most expansive growth opportunities. As it turns out, what I think about an event can totally change my experience of it.

While our thoughts
are caught up in the past
or in the future,
we are missing
the only time
we have to live in:
the present.

Ten thousand flowers in spring,
the moon in autumn,

a cool breeze in summer,
snow in winter.

If your mind isn't clouded
by unnecessary things,

this is the best season of your life.

— WU MEN HUI-K'AI

LOVE IN ACTION

INNER PRACTICE
It's not what we think

At the core of all wisdom traditions is an examination of the habits of the mind.

Don't believe everything you think. Our thoughts come and go, as the Buddhists say, like clouds across an open sky. Suffering happens when we get attached to our thoughts and make them 'real'.

It is helpful to practice this in a quiet place. Sit somewhere comfortably. Notice the sensations in your body. Watch the rise and fall of your breath. Notice when thoughts arise. Be curious about the thought and notice the response this thought has on your body. Recognise, 'I'm having a thought'. Give space around the thought and watch it pass. Return to the simplicity of your present moment experience

What changes with this realisation?

OUTER PRACTICE
Cancer's Message

Feel into the parts of yourself that are most affected by cancer's arrival. There will be parts that are shocked, outraged, afraid, grief-stricken. Honour them all.

Imagine you are visiting the cancer cells in your body. If you were willing to hear, what would cancer have to say to you?

Having heard what cancer has to say, is there anything you wish to reply?

There may be a dialogue that ensues that brings resolution.

How does it feel to be heard?

Be sensitive to other voices that may arise in response to cancer's message. Tread gently and be alert to the needs of those parts that may not have had an opportunity to come forward. You may need to enlist the support of a trained professional to allow their full expression.

Where do I feel trapped, powerless or a victim in relation to my circumstances?

What am I telling myself about my cancer journey?
And what do I make this mean about me?

"We can't choose what happens to us,
but we can choose the meaning we give it."

How might I meet cancer, rather than fight it?
How might I approach my unfolding journey as a result?

Which of the three doors do I habitually choose? Is there one that I prefer?

How could I rewrite my cancer story to empower me?

Owning our story can be hard but not nearly as difficult as spending our lives running from it.

- Brené Brown

What aspects of my life have died and need to be acknowledged, laid to rest and appropriately grieved?

Rest

PART 5

Finding My Power

*"No one saves us but ourselves.
No one can and no one may.
We ourselves must walk our path."*

- Buddha

BRCA

Both my mother and father have had cancer more than once and there are plenty of our extended family members who we've lost to the big 'C'. Several years ago, when my parents and two of my three sisters embarked on genetic testing, they wanted me to do it too. I really didn't want to and asked my family to respect my wishes by not telling me about their results.

I simply did not want the thought that I may actually test positive for the BRCA gene planted in my subconscious, with accompanying nightmare visions of my impending doom rattling around in my fear-prone brain. *Who wants that threatening reality on their life's dashboard? Not me!*

So, when I shared my second diagnosis with my family, my sister could no longer contain the information she held about our family's DNA. She had been withholding this information reluctantly for way too long and now I was going to hear it whether I wanted to or not! I discovered my mother carries the BRCA-1 gene mutation and my father, BRCA-2. Although this sister had tested negative, it seemed I wasn't going to get off so lightly.

I didn't know what to expect. Given my second diagnosis it seemed likely that I may carry one of the genes, though nothing prepared me for the complete shock I felt in discovering I actually have both. Yep, my genetic testing results indicated a positive result for both BRCA-1 and BRCA-2 mutations. Not only that, but neither my breast surgeon, geneticist or oncologist had ever met anyone who carries both. *Am I some sort of freak? Am I doubly doomed?*

SOUL'S SABBATICAL

Discovering I have both BRCA-1 and BRCA-2 really shook my world. I'm not sure if it was the reality of having both genes or discovering this was so rare that none of my medical team had ever met anyone presenting with both.

Questions swirled around my head. *'What did this really mean for me? Am I fated to an outcome determined by my genes?'* Or, *'Is it possible I have some power in this apparently predestined reality?'*

The shock waves kept coming. I felt myself reeling inward, in free-fall again, spiralling deeper and deeper as each diagnosis seemed to crack open yet another of the many layers of my once shiny, polished veneer.

I know I have to stay open to what is being revealed this time, so instead of resisting, I am curious to explore what all this might mean. I'm willing to dive into the darker, deeper places I've always avoided before and get acquainted with myself in ways I never could have done before. I want to understand more fully what is happening within my body, to listen and learn from her depths.

What if my body has an important message for me?
What if I am not limited by my genetic makeup?
What if I have the ability to change my mindset and thus, my life's path?

I believe we are far more than just our physical body. The mind, body and soul are inextricably linked and all play a part in our health and wellbeing. We cannot address what's happening in the body without also considering our physical environment, our emotional landscape and the thoughts and feelings that result.

I see my doctors as my educators and guides into western medicine and their focus is largely on the body and its symptoms. I feel, however, that other aspects of my being are not being considered. I want to truly heal from breast cancer this time, from the inside out and discover the underlying causes, in all dimensions. If I can put an end to this genetic tendency to manifest cancer, I also need to explore the realms of my mind and soul and spirit.

Dr Bruce Lipton, a stem-cell biologist, best-selling author and internationally recognised pioneer for his work in bridging science and spirit, provided valuable insight and hope regarding my situation. In his ground-breaking book The Biology of Belief: Unleashing the Power of Consciousness, Matter & Miracles, Dr Lipton explores the biochemical effects of the brain's function. He asserts that our genes and DNA do not control our body's biology. Instead, our DNA is controlled by signals from outside our cells; or in other words, our cells respond to their environment including the energetic messages emanating from our positive and negative thoughts.

Dr Lipton shows us that our bodies can change as we change our thoughts. In essence, our health is not predestined by our genes, but very much within our control. We have the power to alter our health and well-being for the better.

I had spent many days and weeks lying around, hopelessly wrangling with my thoughts, feeling sorry for myself. My husband was so worried about me, I could see it on his face. It would have been so easy to give up. To quit. Just hand over responsibility for my body to my doctors and accept my fate. However, as I sat looking at my world through a lens of fear, defeat and sadness, a voice was gradually rising up from somewhere within me, reminding me that my medical team could only help me so far and ultimately, I am responsible for my well-being. I am my own wisest healer.

According to the statistics offered by my breast surgeon, I have a 91% chance of survival. That is, if I follow her suggested treatment path of a lumpectomy, 18 rounds of chemotherapy, 20 hits of radiation, Herceptin for a year, a double mastectomy, drug therapy for five years and oh, a hysterectomy too for good measure. This regime feels incredibly daunting and excessive. And all I can think is, if I am going to do ALL of that and it will get me nearly all the way there, what about the remaining 9%? This seems a fairly huge investment of time, money and energy to achieve only 91%.

If I am going to fully meet the cause and the conditions of these cancer cells in my breast and lymph nodes, I believe the key lies in exploring what's beyond the physical. I trust my medical team to take care of removing the physical tumour. However, I made a conscious decision to take full responsibility for the wellbeing of my body, mind and soul and am willing to open to the mystery of their ways.

MY TEACHERS

For as long as I can remember, I have been curious about women's wisdom, personal development, spirituality and the sacred. I have followed many spiritual teachers who have shown me how to access mind and spirit and what I see as the most important pathway to healing myself.

My body may be tired but I have an unquenchable thirst for spiritual knowledge and wisdom. I am eternally grateful to the great teachers who have shown up along my path: Marianne Williamson, Clarissa Pinkola-Estes, Judith Duerk, Brene Brown, Pema Chodron, Carolyn Myss, Byron Katie, Deepak Chopra, Joe Dispenza and Bruce Lipton.

Each in their individual ways have reminded me that I have choices and helped me embody my determination to not only survive but to thrive and live an extraordinary, abundant and soulful existence. A life well lived.

In many ways I feel I have been gifted this time in what I affectionately call my 'Soul's Sabbatical', as a time to rest, to create, to dream. I am so very grateful to be in a position to take this time out, as I was unable to during my first brush with cancer.

Even though my body is yearning for rest, my soul is hungry for growth. I want to understand why cancer has come to visit again and am looking for guidance and insight.

It feels as though my body is giving me this powerful message. It's like my body is the vehicle and cancer a powerful messenger from my soul.

What am I to learn here?
What do I need to let go of?
Can I potentially stop this disease from visiting me, my son and the generations to come?

EASE AND GRACE

Another chemo treatment day arrived. The anxiety and fear had been welling in the days leading up to this, as it always does. I sit impatiently in the reception room waiting for my name to be called and silently cursing them for running late. They're often late. As if it's not already painful enough to sit waiting, the clock ticking loudly on the wall highlights each minute that is delaying the completion of one more treatment, that I can tick off the list and leave behind me. The waiting is awful and I'm seething, anxious, blamey and irrational; not a face I like to show in public.

I am normally so strong. Confidence is one of the protective masks I wear to survive. I often put my feelings aside so I can better handle situations I am presented with, but I couldn't this time. My emotions surged in waves and I felt helpless in this onslaught.

What am I truly fearful of? Ah yes, the v-v-v word … being vulnerable. I have lost so much control over my life and have become so vulnerable, so dependent on the medical staff who have my life in their hands and on my family and friends for support. I hate this feeling of powerlessness.

Because of the COVID-19 pandemic, I am not permitted to have a support person there with me at the clinic for my treatments. I understand why, but this makes me feel even more vulnerable and alone. My inner child is freaking out. She's terrified. She doesn't know what to expect, and like so many unknown situations, there's no way of knowing until you experience it for yourself.

What's going to help me get through this today? How will my body respond?

Deep breaths. Stay calm. Trust in the medical staff. Trust in the chemo drugs they infuse into my body. Trust that I can cope with what is in front me. Trust that my body will take to these drugs well. I must remain positive in my resolve that I will get through this with ease and grace.

That evening following treatment, I was sick as a dog. Chemo and I didn't sit well together, despite my best positive intentions. Every cell of my being was resisting this treatment and most noticeable was the nausea, the flip-flops I felt in my stomach. I started comfort eating in an effort to settle my tummy but nothing seemed to calm the turmoil I felt. It's really hard to keep a positive mindset when my body is full of nausea and pain. I just wanted to quit. Quit this chemo regimen, quit my entire treatment plan and let death take hold. If this was how I was going to feel for the next year, I didn't want it. I just wanted to give up.

Become a student of your journey.

It's been said that when the student is ready, the teacher will appear. Right when I had reached the end of my tether, again, in perfect divine timing, my friend Erin gifted me a book that turned out to be a pivotal turning point in my journey.

HEAL YOURSELF

When I started reading 'Mind over Medicine', by Dr Lissa Rankin, it was like a fresh cold shower shaking me out of my 'victim' story. I did a full pivot in my attitude and jumped into the driver's seat, choosing to listen to my body's wisdom and responding to the directions it was giving me. Rather than giving up, numbing out and being dragged along for the ride, I took responsibility for myself.

I became a student of my journey and started educating myself about my treatment plan. I researched the chemotherapy drugs I was taking, I learned about their side effects and found how I could address them with natural therapies. I started asking more questions of my breast surgeon and oncologist; challenging questions, ones they seemed uncomfortable about and often couldn't answer.

I was claiming responsibility for my body and my health rather than handing the reins over to well-intentioned doctors. I discovered that medical professionals do not like to be challenged and most often have no real interest in treatments beyond their medical training. Suggesting anything outside of this is frowned upon.

I began to see I have the power to heal my own body. The medical fraternity may have been educated from the best schools and hold the best intentions for my wellbeing but I am the one left to pick up the pieces, long after the treatments are over. My doctors are wonderful people with amazing life-saving skills, who do the best they can. The rest is up to me. I am the one who will continue to occupy this dear body of mine, tending to it in recovery as the scars heal, the drugs slowly dissipate from my cells, my hair grows back and organ functions normalise once more. Full healing happens slowly and gradually and it is *my* responsibility to listen, care for and attend to every step in my journey of wellbeing.

You have the power
to change your life
without waiting for someone...

BELIEFS

A placebo is a substance or treatment which has no therapeutic value and is prescribed for the psychological benefit rather than any physical one. They are often in the form of a sugar pill, used as a control when testing the efficacy of new drugs. Given the results, most scientists would not question *whether* placebos work, the only question modern medicine is dealing with is *how* they work.

According to Deepak Chopra MD and Rudolph Tanzi PhD, in their book 'The Healing Self', the reason we still don't have the answer is that most scientists are unwilling to admit that there are intangibles, which they call the 'X Factor', that have a quantifiable effect on health treatment. In their observation, the 'placebo effect' isn't some mysterious response to a sugar pill but rather the robust and measurable effect of three primary components: the body's natural ability to heal, the patient's mindset, and the social context.

Chopra and Tanzi believe that the reason some medicines only work to a certain extent is that some people are 'their own placebos'. That is to say, one's belief in whether they can be healed or not, plays a vital role in the healing process. They found that beliefs, often imprinted since childhood, and even the genes inherited from your parents belong to the X factor and can strongly influence the outcome of any treatment program.

We form many of our beliefs long before we are old enough to consciously choose them for ourselves. Adopted from well-intentioned parents and those in our environment, they often reflect their unresolved wounds, fears and limitations. These **subconscious** beliefs form the foundations of our lives, influencing our experience and driving many of the decisions we make. Rarely are we shown that we can heal spontaneously!

The placebo effect, which brings about healing without any active medical ingredient, offers a very enticing possibility. If you could be 'your own placebo', you would have the safest form of healing at your disposal. Chopra and Tanzi refer to 'the healing self' which according to them, satisfies the real meaning of wholeness. The healing self merges the healer and the healed, turning a patient into a doctor long before a disease ever manifests and therefore, naturally becoming a powerful healer in the presence of illness and disease.

Every cell in your body knows exactly what it needs to restore balance, given the right ingredients. *Could this be true of our body, mind and soul as a whole?* If so, we would only need to contact the level of the self that supports our cells, and consciously offer what is needed.

So, let's accept that our beliefs and our perception of the world are influencing our bodily responses all the time. Most importantly, our beliefs form part of our own unique X Factor and are a key determinant in our body's capacity to heal. We have the power to consciously choose to heal in any given situation, beginning with our choice of beliefs.

Here are some of the most healing beliefs one could hold:

I expect to be happy and well.

I am in control of my health and my life.

Whatever challenge I am faced with, I can handle it.

I feel safe, fearless and resilient.

I have loving friends and family who support me.

I am worthy and loved. I love others too.

I lovingly accept and honour myself.

LOVE IN ACTION

INNER PRACTICE
The Work

Byron Katie has created a process called 'The Work' designed to question what you believe with four simple yet powerful questions. To explore your beliefs is an amazing gift to give yourself. The answers are always inside you, just waiting to be heard.

Ask yourself, who or what upsets you? Why? Recall a specific situation.

To begin, relax and be still. In your mind, re-visit the specific situation where you were angry, hurt, sad, or disappointed with someone. Witness what was happening. Be there now. Notice, name, and feel the emotion you were experiencing at the time. Find the reason you think you were upset.

The Four Questions

Q1. Is it true?

Q2. Can I absolutely know that it's true?

Q3. How do I react, what happens, when I believe that thought?

Q4. Who would I be without that thought?

Turn the thought around to the opposite and the other.
There are worksheets and more information available online at: thework.com

OUTER PRACTICE
Exploring Limiting Beliefs

Beliefs are the thoughts that we think are true. Strung together they create the unquestioned scripts we live by. Until investigated, they can limit our experience and create suffering, often to ourselves and those we love. It is best to keep the beliefs that serve us well and explore those that are causing suffering.

Write down five core limiting beliefs that are holding you back. Consider where each belief originated. For example; life is always hard, our genes determine our health, life is not fair, there's never enough time, I need more money.

_____

_____

_____

_____

_____

_____

_____

_____

_____

_____

_____

_____

It can be very powerful to put these beliefs into the inquiry of The Work. You may well be surprised and delighted with what shows up.

What are my beliefs about my health?

What are my beliefs about my cancer?
Do I have an inkling as to where they may have originated?

Do I believe I am fated to an outcome determined by my genes?

What do I believe about my body's ability to repair itself?

If there was a gift from cancer, what might it be?

What insights am I gaining along my journey so far?

Have I noticed the impact of my beliefs on my healing journey so far?

PART 6

My Body's Wisdom

"The great majority of us are required to
live a life of constant, systematic duplicity.

Your health is bound to be affected by it if,
day after day, you say the opposite of what you feel,
if you grovel before what you dislike and
rejoice at what brings you nothing but misfortune.

Our nervous system isn't just a fiction,
it's part of our physical body, and our soul exists in space
and is inside us, like teeth in our mouth.
It can't be forever violated with impunity."

- Boris Pasternak, Dr Zhivago

GOING DEEPER

There was a snake on our deck yesterday and I thought to look up 'snake' in my animal dreaming cards, and they said…

"a way of gently pointing out that you need to look deep within yourself and honour those aspects that pose the threat of making you ill. We have to hand them over so that we may see clearly again. Snake encourages us to look at our baggage, our burdens and our pain and transmute them into new opportunities and new life. She offers us the chance to physically rebirth ourselves by strengthening us emotionally and deepening our relationship with Spirit."

FORT KNOX

I often found myself locked in my own cage of fear, desperation and disillusion, where my experience of life was getting smaller and smaller. I keep a journal by my bedside and I love the practice of writing my thoughts and feelings, especially when things are going tough. It is so cathartic and has given me such clarity in times when I've needed it most. It's my safe space to explore the deeper aspects of myself.

Today, however, I am feeling resistance to writing. The words just won't flow, or maybe I really don't want to connect with 'that' place that's ugly, hungry, dark. I've ignored whoever is down there most of my life and am beginning to pay the price. Her voice is getting louder now, demanding to be heard. She's got something important to say.

Do I really want to hear it?

When I scratch at the first layer, my first feeling in response is sadness, so much sadness. So, I sit with that. The familiar sad feelings I know so well … But what sits behind my sadness? If I were to sink into it and go deeper, what might sadness be a cover for?

Before I can even get in there, I must acknowledge what separates my outer world from my inner one. It's a protective wall constructed to keep me safe, or so I thought. It's built of the thickest stone, very high and very well guarded. It's my Fort Knox.

Very few people are permitted beyond it. If I let them inside, they would see what's been hidden; my underbelly of fear, guilt, shame, the belief that I am not enough, that I am not worthy.

My logical mind knows this isn't 'real' and can rationalise this, but the little girl that resides in the fort of her own making is wounded. She has been shut down, stomped on and cast aside. She is too much and she's not enough. She is ugly and she is beautiful. She is loving and she is a bitch, fighting to protect herself.

Her wounds are deep and still unhealed. She has been betrayed too many times by those she loved most. She longed to be loved, to be held, to know she is enough. She sought refuge in superficial relationships with people who could never fill that aching need within her longing heart.

As I travel down this path, I wonder if every conversation, every event, every thought has brought me right here, right now; to this place where my outer and inner worlds have collided. My thick fortress has begun to crumble and there is a faint light shining through the cracks.

It's taken all this time and all this suffering to bring me here and perhaps, it is time to venture inward and get acquainted with her. To go within and really see myself, to truly accept me for me. To reconcile past betrayals. To forgive, to make peace.

GRIEVING

I am almost a week post chemo treatment and still feeling low. As much as I can and 'should' be getting on with my day and tasks, I am resisting. I am tired. I am bored as hell. I am frustrated. And I'm sad. I am feeling so much loss; the loss of my health, my freedom, my independence, my social connection, my sense of self, my identity, my self-image. In the space of three months, my life is virtually unrecognisable.

I have become a hermit, a captive in my own home, a dependent now reliant on Chris to do our shopping and chauffeur me to medical appointments. What happened to the independent, go-getter I used to be? Where did she go?

There's so much grief welling up, grief for the life I once lived, grief for the person I once was, for the hair and eyelashes I have taken for granted all these years.

My grief feels thick and heavy, like I'm wading through molasses. Each step requires effort and energy I don't have. I am dead tired, beyond exhausted and I want nothing more than to feel sorry for myself. I'm wallowing in pity for the life that now surrounds me. I just want to stay feeling this shitty … and be left in peace.

As I look out my window another stunning day of blue sky and sunshine beams back at me. I can hear the birds chirping their happy song and I try to force a smile to see if that will lift my spirits, but sadness has settled in, colouring everything grey, flat and lifeless.

I have so much to be grateful for. How can I waste even one minute of this day feeling sorry for myself when the weather is so damn glorious? I 'should' be outside making the most of this perfect day. Chris is being so supportive and desperately trying to cheer me up. I know he's trying his best but nothing can shift the dark cloud that bears down on me now.

Am I going crazy? Why am I feeling so flat?

ROCK BOTTOM

I yearned to feel happy again, feel anything on the positive end of the spectrum, but it was as though I had forgotten how to feel that way anymore. I was struggling, really struggling. I found it difficult to accept my current situation. I had so many emotions swirling through me, I couldn't manage, or cope.

I felt lonely and isolated from the world. There were plenty of people I could reach out to but I didn't feel like talking to anyone. I didn't think they'd understand. I didn't want to burden them with my messiness anyway. I was drowning in it.

I had hit rock bottom and knew I needed help. Yes, this independent, 'I've got this' chick had hit rock bottom and needed support - not from my husband, not from my friends, but from someone who could validate and normalise my cancer experience.

The next morning, I told Chris I needed help. He looked up the phone number for the Cancer Council and started dialling. He introduced himself and explained that he was ringing on my behalf, then handed the phone over to me to speak with a nurse counsellor.

Lucy had a lovely and compassionate voice and disarming way of making me feel safe and cared for. I shared with her the turbulence of my year so far, my diagnosis, the cancellation of our wedding celebrations, shutting down my business, having a lumpectomy, COVID-19 pandemic and going into self-imposed isolation, commencing chemo and losing my hair. As I shared how much had happened so rapidly, I was struck by just how much change I had endured. Somehow by hearing myself speaking all this change out loud, brought all of my hurt and pain to the surface. I could hear the cracking in my voice and the heat rising in my body and knew I couldn't hold it in any longer. I surrendered to the sweet release that came as the tears began to flow. Lucy knew what I was going through. She had heard similar stories many times before. She understood, she felt my pain and was just the balm I needed.

Finally, the full extent of the cataclysmic shifts in my life hit me like a ton of bricks. I know I am strong and resilient but THIS is a lot for anyone to handle and it was so good to be able to acknowledge it, to feel it and let it all out.

DEATH

Throughout life there are cycles that complete, whether we choose them or not. Relationships end, children leave home, a job is left or a diagnosis of breast cancer changes everything. We don't always notice it at the time, but these transitions, or deaths are constant in life. Whether radical and sudden or imperceptibly subtle, there are moments when we realise, life will never be the same and there is a 'dying' of what once was and will never be again.

For me, one of those moments was seeing my son move out and start university. Don't get me wrong, there was part of me that was singing from the rooftops about my newfound freedom and with a maternal desire to see him spread his wings. Another part of me however, was filled with sadness. There was grieving for what we shared, knowing that our relationship will never be the same, that my baby had become an adult. Yes, all a part of life's journey, but a death just the same.

How did I learn to override life's natural rhythm and neglect these powerful points of change, to take pause and allow time to grieve? It's understandable, given our cultural propensity to judge sorrow as 'weakness', to avoid pain and keep moving, no matter the cost to the soul. I am on unfamiliar ground, as there are so many unacknowledged endings and my heart is heavy.

For me, my breast cancer diagnosis is another death. I am dying to the healthy, vibrant, fearless woman I once was and having to embrace a whole new set of priorities; absorbing medical information, attending endless appointments and undergoing a relentless treatment plan that takes my whole attention.

My, how life can shift on a dime!

Life
is a series of
deaths.

To discover who she is,
a woman must descend into her own depths.

She must leave the safe role of remaining a faithful daughter of the collectives around her and descend to her individual feeling values. It will be her task to experience her pain ... the pain of her own unique feeling values calling to her, pressing to emerge.

To discover who she is, a woman must trust the places of darkness where she can meet her own deepest nature and give it voice ... weaving the threads of her life into a fabric to be named and given ... sharing it with the women around her as she comes to a true and certain sense of herself.

- JUDITH DUERK: *A CIRCLE OF STONES*

ACHIEVING

The past few days have been really challenging for me. I have felt pretty lousy both physically and emotionally. I have never liked the word 'depression' and feel it is often misused, but I actually have a glimpse of what people must experience when they are diagnosed 'depressed'. The sun was shining, the birds were chirping, the world continued to spin but all I could feel was grey. Lifeless. Nothing could lift me from my self-pity party for one and I had no motivation to move at all.

My wise friend Leonie once said we aren't taught how to sit with our pain or our difficult and 'negative' emotions. In fact, we are conditioned from a young age to cheer up, toughen up and just get on with things. We have become highly skilled at avoiding painful feelings like: sadness, grief, loss and fear. For many of us, we bypass the uncomfortable with the pleasurable distraction of alcohol, drugs, food, medication, sex and endless entertainment. You will have your own favourite methods!

Feeling flat as a tack, coupled with the self-imposed exile given our current COVID pandemic, it was as though life had delivered me the perfect storm. Nothing to do. Nowhere to go. Nowhere to hide. I was left with no option but to sit smack dab in the middle of my own shit storm. There was literally NOTHING to divert my attention, or escape how I was feeling. It was sheer torture.

I sat on the couch day after day, week after week feeling a level of frustration I hadn't experienced before. I wanted so much to be up and about and getting shit done; striving, producing and achieving. In my world, there is nothing more gratifying than getting things ticked off my to-do list. It makes me feel productive, worthy, alive.

As I battled with my old habitual patterns of 'doing', some new thoughts were arising.

Who am I when I am not achieving?
What would it be like to just 'be'?
Why is just 'being' so darn uncomfortable?

I like to contribute. I like to do my share. I like to give and help others. It makes me feel worthwhile. It's how I have defined myself; a doer, a get-shit-done girl. *But for what purpose? What is motivating me to be this way? Who, if anyone, am I trying to impress?*

Images of my mother come to me; the stoic, hard-working woman humbly raising four daughters and keeping her household in tip-top shape. In my view, that was her role, her job description, her duty and she did it perfectly. She kept her home and the family running smoothly, all the while modelling what a 'good' mother and housewife should be.

A GOOD MOTHER

Make sure everyone else's needs are taken care of. Check.

Feed the children, get them dressed and off to school. Check.

Have dinner ready, bathe the children and get them to bed. Check.

Repeat. Check.

Make sure the house is clean and presentable. Check.

Mend the clothes. Bake some bread. Check.

Iron his shirts. Pack his lunches and take care of your husband's needs. Check.

Give, give, give. Check.

Tend to your needs but only if there is time left at the end of the day. Check.

The underlying message: Be of service. Be a martyr. Give, give, give.

My mother modelled this beautifully for all of us. The behavioural patterns are well ingrained, the neural pathways set.

UNRAVELLING

We are complicated beings, aren't we?

Until I began to see some of my habitual patterns, I lived my life as though on auto-pilot; giving, giving, giving. Giving away the energy I should have been conserving for my own ever-diminishing energy reservoir. Why am I doing this to myself? Why do I value and place the needs of others so much higher than my own? I wondered what drove this behaviour? Was I trying to impress someone? My parents, my husband, my girlfriends?

I recall my first brush with breast cancer and how tired and unproductive I was as I recovered from my lumpectomy surgery. Family and friends were shocked and found it difficult to relate to me when not the usual 'achieving' me. I was met with, 'Oh you're not working?', 'You don't have energy to do much?', 'Well, what are you doing with yourself?' I've always been a high achiever. It is what I was rewarded for and encouraged to do. It is how I had always defined myself and others hadn't seen anything other than this well-polished identity.

Unravelling my innate drive to achieve at all costs will take some undoing.

Nothing to strive for
No need to struggle
Let go of the 'shoulds'
Surrender to what is now…

GRATITUDE

Despite the grief, sadness and loss that pervade my life now, I marvel at the well of gratitude within me too. Like two sides of a coin, I can feel the weightiness of grief and at the same time am also so, so grateful for the gifts in all of it.

Merryn once said that there will be a silver lining in all of this for me. She says, 'We don't deliberately create dis-ease, there is always a positive intent for it and in some way, I will get what I really need from this.' I think she might be right.

I have manifested the opportunity to stop, to let down my guard and stop trying to control everything. I've learned to be vulnerable and express myself more authentically. I am allowing myself to be held and supported by others, to surrender, receive … and just BE.

It only took me 49 years and two breast lumps to truly 'get' this message and make space for it to land. Message received. Thank you.

Happiness will never come
to those who fail to appreciate
what they already have.

- BUDDHA

FEELING IS HEALING

In modern 'civilised' culture, we aren't taught emotional literacy; how to become familiar with these feeling states and to value the insights our emotional bodies carry. Instead, our culture has a preference for 'numbing out' uncomfortable emotions with infinite distractions. Caffeine, alcohol, drugs, cigarettes, TV, sex, food, work etc., keep us distanced from our feelings and able to 'carry on' business as usual. The cumulative effect is often a lifetime of repressed, unresolved emotions sitting densely in our bodies.

Confession: I have spent much of my life feeling like a passenger, disassociated from my feelings, living on the surface and reactive to my environment. If I am really honest with myself, I've totally avoided any painful emotions and placated myself with a wide range of pleasures.

PERMISSION TO FEEL

Though many people take great pride in 'managing' or rather repressing their emotions, denying them altogether is not humanly possible.

The first thing you did when you arrived in this world was cry. You have and will cry many times throughout your life, and when you depart you will likely leave a lot of people crying. Under the tough armour we use for protection, we are feeling, sensitive beings who love and hurt and feel an amazing range of emotional experiences. That's part of being human.

With that said, your emotional world may not be the usual place you occupy in your life. You may be a practical, take-charge, get-things-done type of woman like me, who is generally very steadfast and grounded ... *but you still have an emotional world.*

The sensations and feelings in your body are always there, circulating and influencing every thought, decision and behaviour. Owning that you are an emotional being and validating those feelings that don't always make sense is the first step towards connecting with the wisdom of your emotional body.

Yes, it is sometimes painful, and can be overwhelming when allowing the pent up feelings their expression, but your courage in being willing to feel, and not think your way through this unfamiliar language of the soul, is an essential step on the path towards wholeness.

LOVE IN ACTION

INNER PRACTICE
Befriending Your Body

This practice is to help build your awareness of the wisdom in your body and to gradually build capacity in your nervous system to be with whatever arises.

Be still for 60 seconds. Breathe 3 deep breaths.

Take a few moments to really feel into your body, notice what's there and then feel into these questions:

What am I feeling in my body right now? What qualities am I feeling? How is it to sit with that and notice what changes?

Where do I feel disharmony or discomfort? How is it to sit with it? Are the feelings pleasant, neutral or uncomfortable? Is this a recurring feeling?

What thoughts and information come as I sit with this? Notice if it changes.

Stay with this as long as you can without causing stress. Be playful and curious.

Notice anything that may have changed for you.

OUTER PRACTICE
Feeling is Healing

We receive communication from our emotional body through our feelings. The human experience includes feeling a wide range of emotions and at times those emotions can get stuck in our body. We aren't taught to be comfortable with feeling and expressing these emotions. Here are some ways to help feel our emotions so we can release them.

1. Find a quiet space away from others and free from distraction. Allow around 5 minutes. Take a regular sized bath towel and roll it tightly to make a log shape. Connect with any pent-up emotional charge you wish to clear and ground yourself before commencing this practice.

Bend your knees slightly, take a deep breath and on the exhale, take a big swing with the towel roll and whack it down on a bed/chair repeatedly to release built up tension. Feel free to express yourself verbally with this exercise too. Yelling and screaming are perfect for letting go.

After a few rounds, stop and take notice of what's happening in your body. You may choose to lie on the bed or ground to fully release and feel the spaciousness inside.

2. If it's difficult to connect with an emotion, having a visual cue may help. Try watching a film that connects you with the feelings you'd like to arouse or release. e.g., a sad film to release sadness.

3. Create a Spotify music playlist that helps you arouse feelings you'd like to evoke or release. Perhaps, you could create a soundtrack to your journey.

You can find my Spotify playlists 'Feeling is Healing' to feel more deeply and 'Dance it Up' to lift your spirits or 'Soulful Sundays' to bring more calm.

The body never lies.

– MARTHA GRAHAM

Who am I when I'm not achieving?
What would it be like to just 'be'?

How am I really feeling at this very moment?

How comfortable am I to stay present with my fear and uncertainty without distracting myself?

Where am I longing to use my voice, to speak up?

What is it I long to say but as yet haven't had the courage or confidence?

Where in my life do I need to stop asking other people what they think, and trust my own inner wisdom?

Which parts of myself do I need to reclaim to come home to myself?
Who was I before everyone else told me who to be?

If I were to write a letter of love to myself… what would it say?

Slow Way Down

Spring

PART 7

My Inner Sanctuary

"Within you, there is a stillness and a sanctuary to which you can retreat at any time and be yourself."

- Herman Hesse

SEISMIC SHOCK

I was speaking to a lady who was diagnosed with breast cancer some five years ago. Her doctor delivered this news in a rather cold, clinical and uncompassionate way, as is unfortunately the case for so many women. Her diagnosis arrived on the back of two other significant losses in her life which she was still grieving, and receiving the news in such an abrupt manner, resulted in her literally collapsing on the doctor's floor. The cumulative impact of these traumas was simply too much for her system to handle.

Although I didn't collapse on the floor, both my first and second diagnosis came as a seismic shock, evoking a range of responses and emotions I couldn't control. My mouth went dry and I'm pretty sure my heart stopped beating for a bit. As the tears streamed down my face, I was met with the reality of a diagnosis that is so much bigger than me. I wasn't prepared for it and I had no idea how to deal with it. For the first time in my life, I felt truly out of control. There was no quick fix to address these rogue cells growing inside me and all I wanted to do was curl up under a blanket and hope the whole thing just went away.

On reflection, my nervous system literally shut-down to protect itself. I was numb and couldn't feel my body and everything seemed vague and floaty. I lacked the awareness whilst in the storm but the truth was, I was a red-hot mess unable to fully comprehend my situation, take in information about my health and the proposed treatment plan or make a sensible decision to save myself.

I was in shock. I was scared. I feared for my life.

RESPONDING TO STRESS

Our autonomic nervous system (ANS) plays a vital role in responding to stress through its main branches: the sympathetic nervous system and the parasympathetic nervous system. They operate in an amazingly sophisticated way, orchestrating our response to both internal and external stimuli. There is a wealth of information available, some of it in the References section at then end of this journal, though I want to just outline the basics here as it was so helpful for me to understand that my responses to my radically altered life situation were natural, human and did not mean I was losing the plot!

The limbic system and the brain stem (sometimes called the reptilian brain) are the oldest parts of our brain and govern our survival. These primitive systems are entirely subconscious and are designed to keep us safe and out of harm's way. When under stress, in perceived or actual threat, the brain will instantly send neuro-chemical signals to our muscles, nerves and organs as the body prepares to protect itself, it will automatically choose the mode most available to the circumstances.

This is called the 'fight, flight or freeze' response. There are other subtle survival responses, but we will stay with the primary ones for now. We will choose to 'fight' in situations that appear beatable, 'flight' if there's an advantage is escaping and opt to 'freeze' when the situation is just too large and overwhelming. The primitive brain carries the learned behaviour of our animal ancestors, understanding that feigning death, shutting down most systems, slowing of the heart rate and breath, the cold, still appearance of being lifeless, could signal to a predator that they were already dead and not worth pursuing. Once the threat had passed, the animal would slowly come out of 'freeze', breathing deeply, shaking itself off and running back into its life without carrying any residue of the encounter.

The big difference between animals in a natural state and our modern human response, is that we almost universally carry the burden of unresolved trauma and the stresses of living at an unrealistic pace, out of sequence with our natural rhythms, not respecting the need for rest and reparation as equal to the need for connection and stimulation.

PERCEPTION

Did you know that our brain can't actually tell the difference between a real and perceived threat? The circuits that are activated in the brain and the nervous system are identical, whether the stimulus comes from 'reality' in the outside environment, or from inside, as a thought or memory. As an example, imagine a friend played a trick on you and placed a plastic snake in your path. At first sight, your sympathetic nervous system might go into high-alert as your brain believes the plastic snake is a real one and you will head straight into a 'fight, flight or freeze' response. Once the neocortex (the area responsible for critical analysis, rational decision making) recognises it is merely a toy snake and of no real threat to you, your system will release the energy that has been activated in a variety of ways. You might sweat, go cold, feel weak and dizzy, spontaneously shake or twitch, sigh and even emotionally express to release the tension. Fainting is possible too!

The sympathetic nervous system is the branch of the nervous system responsible for arousal, excitation, appetite and movement. Once activated, cortisol and adrenaline levels increase in our body and in a balanced system, these responses are well regulated and will return back to normal, once the need for action or the threat has passed. This branch of the ANS is necessary for our survival because it enables us to respond quickly to avoid potential threats.

Conversely, the parasympathetic nervous system is the branch often referred to as the 'rest and digest' function. It releases dopamine, serotonin, endorphins and oxytocin, the pleasure chemicals. It generates a feeling of relaxation and calm in the mind and helps the body to restore health, fall into sleep and repair injury. This function is often referred to as 'down-regulation', the soothing and calming and settling after excitation and arousal.

The two systems work together; as one becomes more active the other becomes less active in a kind of wave motion, normally within a 'window of tolerance' that meets the natural rhythm of needs for arousal and relaxation in our daily lives. However, when operating in constant stress, or with layers of unresolved or complex trauma, they can get out of balance and stay 'stuck' predominantly in one mode or the other. One extreme being a kind of mania, in fear and avoiding any real feeling; the other can look like inertia, depression and chronic ill-health.

Both come with real costs to our quality of life; our capacity for learning and assimilating new information, retaining memories and engaging in healthy social relationships can be impaired. The diminishment of our joy, enthusiasm and creativity is often slow, gradual and undetected as we find ourselves at some point, with life energy depleted and silently eroded by the daily grind of living.

HIGH ALERT

With our fast-paced, sensory overloaded, never-enough-time lifestyle, I'd suggest that the majority of us are living in a constant state of stress, on high alert and habitually anxious with the sympathetic nervous system in a constant state of arousal, even though there's no immediate real threat. I know this was the case for me, anyway. I used to be an adrenaline junky, filling my days with way more than I could handle in the pursuit of achievement and wearing my 'I'm so busy' label like it was some badge of honour. I was literally wearing myself out. I was my own biggest hazard to my health and happiness!

So, when my second breast cancer diagnosis arrived, my sympathetic nervous system was already on high-alert, I was exhausted and unable to process this very real threat on top of everything else I had going on. I went into a state of 'freeze' immediately. I went into overwhelm, I went numb and wanted to disappear. And the logical part of my brain literally shut-down at a time in my life when I needed it most.

Many of us are familiar with how a fight or flight response feels in our body. However do you know what a freeze response feels like?

Signs of the 'freeze' response:

- Your muscles may lock up
- You may have feelings of numbness, detachment or disassociation
- You may feel overwhelmed
- You may feel cold, stuck or trapped
- You may have a sense of stiffness or heaviness
- You may hold your breath involuntarily
- You may feel like shrinking or trying to disappear

ADDICTED TO STRESS

I realised these two branches of my ANS were completely out of balance. I only had one speed and that was flat-out. I continually told myself that I thrived on the 'busy-ness' and by meeting deadlines but the truth of it was that I was running on empty and wasn't taking the time to re-fuel. Ongoing stress literally shuts off the capacity to process information effectively and make sound decisions and I had no idea I was operating in a kind of addictive cycle that produced a cocktail of stimulating chemicals, giving me a 'high' but without the balance of rest, reflection and integration. It took this major wake-up call to reassess the environment I was subjecting my dear body to and it was going to take some reprogramming and a detox from the habits of a lifetime.

Nature does not hurry,
yet everything is accomplished.

- LAO TZU

FINDING CALM

The good news is that we can consciously activate the parasympathetic nervous system, in a variety of simple ways to calm our nerves and restore balance. With that balance restored, we are better able to cope with a life-threatening diagnosis, make better decisions about our way forward and ensure that our bodily systems continue to work in harmony for optimal health.

KNOWING WHAT BRINGS YOU COMFORT IS A BEAUTIFUL EXERCISE IN SELF-CARE.

Meditation can often slow down the stress response and calm the body, however it is important to have skilled guidance with your practise, as sometimes meeting the long-held distress in the body can be re-traumatising and can overwhelm the system. It is really good to find a trusted somatic practitioner or meditation teacher to advise you before beginning a regular practise.

As I progressed through treatment, I started noticing the activities that gave me comfort and helped me to calm my nerves and bring a sense of balance.

These are my favourite ways to practice self-care:

- Creative expression in my journal, drawing or colouring in
- Applying or diffusing calming and peaceful essential oils
- A warm bubble bath with lit candles and beautiful music
- A walk along the beach (barefoot) or forest-bathing in the woods
- A call with a girlfriend who can hold space for me
- A lovely cup of calming tea like chai, chamomile or earl grey
- Reading a favourite book
- Spending time propagating plants or tending to my garden
- A hug from someone close to me, or a cuddle with a pet
- Spend time with people I love and who nourish my soul
- Book in for an exquisite, relaxation massage or facial
- Listen to relaxation or yogic music or attend a sound-healing session
- Take a restful nap with a soft blanket

What practices bring you calm and soothe your soul?

Rest
isn't what you do at the end of your life,
no matter what the gravestones say.

It is something you do in order to
live deeply and well.

It looks like 'nothing' only to those radiated
by rickety histories and fluorescent memories.

May it be that your rest has that kind of
nourishing darkness, and your darker days
have that kind of fuller rest.

— STEPHEN JENKINSON

Here are some techniques for stimulating your parasympathetic nervous system that you can try anywhere, anytime.

Meditative breathing
Breathe from your diaphragm. Take long, slow, deep breaths. This stimulates the parasympathetic nervous system because it slows down your breathing. If you put your hand on your stomach and it rises up and down slightly as you breathe, you know you're breathing from your diaphragm or abdomen.

Combine diaphragmatic breathing and mindfulness
Try diaphragmatic breathing in conjunction with mindfulness; the practice of simply resting your attention on something that is happening in the present moment. If your sympathetic nervous system is in a constant state of arousal, mindfulness helps restore the proper balance between the sympathetic and parasympathetic systems. This usually creates a feeling of calm and relaxation.

Imagery
Use imagery to stimulate the parasympathetic nervous system. Visualise yourself in a peaceful place, like near a mountain stream, a forest, a secluded beach. Engage all your senses in this imagery; take in the sights, sounds, the feel of the breeze on your face and track any changes in your present time experience.

Laughter
Don't underestimate the power of a good belly laugh. Laughter is a great way to take your mind off stressful situations as it naturally releases tension. The muscles involved in the smile on the face, the change in breathing and belly shaking are all connected to the vagus nerve, which activates the parasympathetic nervous system and brings calm.

Mono-Tasking
The desire to get many things done simultaneously can be attractive, with the rush of chemicals associated with momentum and accomplishment and whilst it is sometimes necessary, try mono-tasking. This is the art of doing one thing at a time, deliberately and slowly. Traditional meditation practice often asks us to be 'mindful' of everything involved in simply walking, or doing simple daily tasks. This is a very challenging approach for me and one I need to employ deep breathing techniques to achieve!

Social Connection
Surrounding yourself with loved ones, having genuine connection and physical touch is a basic human need. We co-regulate each other's nervous systems and being close to those we love can literally make us feel better and soul-nourished.

Body Care
Moving the body is not only good practice, it's a great way to oxygenate the blood, engage our parasympathetic nervous system and bring balance. Try gentle exercise in a form that you enjoy, do some stretching or have a relaxation massage and see how your body responds.

LOVE IN ACTION

INNER PRACTICE
Finding Calm

1. Sit or lie quietly in a comfortable position.

2. Close your eyes.

3. Choose a focus word, short phrase, or prayer that is aligned to your belief system. You might use 'Peace, The Lord is My Shepherd, Hail Mary, Shalom, Om or Love'. My favourite is one that my psychologist Tracey inspired me to use: 'Profound Peace'.

4. Place one hand on your heart and the other on your belly (womb) or place one hand on your forehead and the other on the back of your neck. Take a moment to feel the sensations in your hands, as well as the place on your body receiving your touch. This physical connection with yourself will bring calm and a sense of safety.

5. Breathe slowly and naturally, and as you do, say your focus word, sound, phrase or prayer silently to yourself, or out loud as you exhale. Feel the vibration of your voice in your body.

6. Stay here as long as you like. 10-20 minutes is ideal. My best times to do this practice are just as I wake up in the morning or before going to bed at night.

Body Scan Meditation

Meditation is one of the most valuable tools I used to keep sane, grounded and calm throughout my cancer journey. Instead of comfort-eating (as I couldn't tolerate many foods!) I found comfort-meditating much more satisfying.

I have created a number of meditations to help you through the days and months ahead. Try the 'Body Scan' meditation or any of the others which resonate with you.

OUTER PRACTICE

In some ways, I took on my healing journey like a special project. I was determined to do everything and anything in my power to be more calm, relaxed and healthy during and beyond my treatment.

When my energy allowed, I tried to do some of my favourite activities which I knew would support and sustain me during this challenging time. Despite feeling lethargic and down at times, some of the activities that helped to get me moving, keep my muscles active and lift my spirits were things like:

Yoga - my favourite during treatment was yin yoga as I was low on energy but loved stretching. Try any gentle yoga class.

Body Balance - I just love this blended class of tai chi, pilates and yoga created by Les Mills. It is a choreographed class to blissful music. There are plenty of free classes available on youtube or you can buy an online low-cost membership and do these classes at home.

Qigong - is a self healing exercise practice with roots in Chinese medicine involving moving meditation, slow-flowing movement and deep breathing to nourish our life force energy or chi. This is a great class to invigorate your energy. There are plenty of free classes on youtube or seek out a recommended teacher who can guide you and custom-build a sequence to suit your particular circumstance.

EFT - or Emotional Freedom Technique is an alternative treatment for physical pain and emotional distress. It's also referred to as tapping or psychological acupressure. People use this technique to reduce physical and emotional pain and balance their energy system.

I introduced this self-care ritual in the shower each morning.

Try gently tapping yourself a few times in each of the following locations and repeat to yourself, 'I love and accept myself' simultaneously.

Eyebrows, side of eyes, under eyes, under nose, chin, collarbones, thymus (upper chest), under left arm, underside of left wrist.

Repeat this practice for a total of three rounds.

For more information and resources on EFT, check out my website.

You are the greatest project you will ever work on.

Soulful Conversations - probably the thing that helped me most was surrounding myself with loved ones who could hold space for me and be okay as I fell apart. There is nothing another person can fix in such moments but companionship and compassion are key. I also found a couple of amazing therapists along the way who were well read and deeply spiritual who gave me great comfort and helped normalise my experience.

Dancing - dancing is just great fun! I certainly didn't feel like being out in the world during this time so I created some fun spotify playlists and danced and sang at the top of my lungs around the house. The movement and vibrational force of my voice were incredibly therapeutic.

Painting - I started tapping into some of my creativity and got the paint brushes out. Thinking there was a 'right' way to paint, I did complete an online course to give me some guidance but quickly was on my way to creating my own masterpieces.

What physical practices soothe and calm you? Are there others that empower and enliven you?

What am I noticing in my body?

Am I carrying any tension?

What do I habitually do when I feel tense?

What am I noticing with my breath?

What's happening with my feelings?

What's happening with my thoughts?

What are some other practices that I could try?

What activities nourish me and help bring me calm?

What people, habits and obligations keep me from prioritising myself?
What could I be doing to cultivate my inner sanctuary?

Just Be

PART 8
Trusting My Soul's Plan

*"Trust that your soul has a plan
and even if you can't see it all,
know that everything will unfold
as it is meant to."*

- Deepak Chopra

CHURCH

When I was young, our family went to church every Sunday without exception. My sisters and I were encouraged to put on our best clothes, our best behaviour and biggest smiles and off we went to demonstrate to the minister and church congregation that we were good, holy and the perfect family.

I sat on the wooden pew, admiring the coloured light coming through the stained glass windows and singing hymns at the top of my lungs as though God could hear me, and I felt the incongruence even then.

As I grew into my teens, I learned that going to church was actually compulsory in my family and that I really had no choice in the matter. If I expressed my frustration or disappointment about this, the requirement for my attendance at church grew stronger! And so did my resistance to playing the part of the 'good' girl or wanting any relationship with God at all. I did what any hormone activated teenager would do, I rebelled!

My rebellion played out in a number of ways. I started looking outside the constraints of home for excitement and stimulation, playing with alcohol and boys, the things I knew would get the most reaction from my parents. I grew angry at the whole notion of God and refused to accept that God played any part in my life. I projected the frustration I felt onto my parents, and turned my back on God. As soon as I turned 18, I moved out of home and never went to church again.

It was around this same time that a deep sadness took hold within me. I felt a loneliness and disconnection that was inconsolable. I tried to relieve this sadness with love, or what I took for love. Love from the wrong sort of men. Love from the stimulation of travels and adventures, from food and all manner of pleasures, people and places that could never fill the void I felt deep inside.

I kept going on this treadmill, despite the harrowing sense of emptiness, until one day a friend suggested that my ubiquitous sadness might very well be a feeling of separation from God, the Divine, Source, Mother Earth or whatever name you give that 'Otherness' that inter-connects us all and makes unquestionable sense of things.

You can imagine my shock, disappointment and refusal to accept this as my truth. I had been managing just fine on my own thank you very much! At least that was what I told myself … but my inner wisdom knew immediately a truth had been spoken.

At 49 years old, I was confronted with the truth that the void I felt in every cell of my body was actually an undeniable longing for a connection to God, the Divine, to my higher self, to something greater than me.

We're like snow globes,
creating a flurry around us,
distracting us
so we never have to face
the truth within us.

- GLENNON DOYLE

I don't like to use the term 'God' as it reminds me of the religion that was once forced upon me by well-intentioned parents and my refusal to accept that form of higher power as an ally in my life. I prefer the term the 'Divine' as this feels more feminine, loving and energetically inclusive.

So my journey to connect with the Divine began when I had the maturity to see things with fresh eyes and an impetus that was much more life threatening than my first diagnosis.

MY TRUTH

How do you unlearn patterns that are so deeply entrenched in your foundational beliefs about who you are? How do you find love for something you have refused to believe in your whole life? Confronted with a second diagnosis and connecting with deeper, darker parts of myself, I began to investigate, question and explore a lifetime of patterns that no longer served me.

In the ancient Hawaiian practice of Ho'oponopono used to clear negativity from one's thoughts, I learned that having faith is the pathway to joy, happiness and inspiration. To let go and let God as they say.

When I went to church, paradoxically, I felt separate from the Divine. I felt like the Divine was something external to me and that I had to go to this special building to access Her. For me, the truth is that the Divine is all around us as much as She is within us. We are all Divine beings. So connecting to Her doesn't require a visit to a local church as much as it does to connect to the knowing within you.

It felt like I was choosing myself rather than the Divine when attending church but in fact, it was the other way around. I chose to honour myself *and* the Divine, instead of church, which sat so much better with me.

LIFE'S CHALLENGES

From an early age, I have been a fatalist. I believed that as much as we have free will, there is also a divine path uniquely set out for each of us; a path of lessons and challenges that lead to enlightenment and wholeness, should we choose it. I started to see every person that crossed my path as someone I was meant to meet who had a pearl of wisdom I needed. I started getting curious about opportunities that presented and wondered if this was where I was meant to go. I began to trust that literally everything is working out for my soul's growth and for my highest good.

Let go and let God.

Today

I am remembering who I am.
I am love. I am light.
I am divine. I am safe.
I am grounded. I am the Universe
And the Universe is me.
I am all that is.

#Moonomens

I see the many challenges I've experienced in my life, including cancer, as experiences that are divinely ordered to assist me in embodying my highest potential. I'm seeing there is a rhyme and reason for everything that shows up.

I began to observe my life from more of an objective position, as though I was watching it from high above. Every challenge: moving overseas, having a son, enduring a divorce, ending a partnership, losing a job, were each a defining moment and I could choose to sink or swim.

Even though these were some of the most challenging days of my life, on reflection they were also the events that provided me with the most growth and have tangibly helped shape the person I have become.

HAVE FAITH

In Marianne Williamson's words, 'We all have faith … faith in possibility or faith that that possibility doesn't exist.'

Or in other words, we have faith in the power of cancer to kill us or faith in the power of the Divine's infinite force to make miracles manifest.

Sitting in the depths of my own darkest days and nights of my soul, when I just wanted to give up, that quieter voice within me grew stronger. I decided to give her voice an audience and heeded her advice. My deepest instinct is to survive. I so very much want to live, not just on autopilot but I want to live an extraordinarily abundant, rich and wonderful life. I know for certain that I am not ready to leave this earth and I am prepared to do what it takes to heal at all levels.

I intuitively knew that I would achieve this in a new and exciting way. After all, what I had been doing wasn't working for me! It was time to do things differently.

I trusted a force greater than me would hold and support me through this. I also wanted to tap into that infinite well within me that kept telling me I was going to be okay, if only I would listen.

No mud, no lotus.

– THICH NHAT HANH

Faith
is taking the first step
even when you don't see
the whole staircase.

- MARTIN LUTHER KING JR

DIVINE MOMENTS

So how do I actually get to dwell in those quiet moments that have eluded me my entire life? How do I make space to listen and truly hear my inner voice and what she has to say? Perhaps these were the very moments I have been running from my whole life as I filled my days with endless tasks and unfulfilling relationships.

The first step is creating time and space for quiet to show itself; to be still, honour my inner knowing, give her voice and be receptive to her suggestions.

Before my diagnosis, there was very little quiet time in my schedule. I didn't value it so I didn't make time for it. It was as simple as that. Even during my chemo treatment, when all my work commitments had disappeared, I found my schedule getting busy once again. Medical appointments, exercise, therapy, reading, zoom catch-ups with friends started filling my days leaving me tired and disconnected.

The art of saying no and asserting loving boundaries was key to my healing journey and creating the space for stillness. I started experiencing divine moments in the shower, while driving my car, while writing in my journal. I received glimpses of inspiration, as though my soul was suggesting what I should do next. It wasn't like a voice or an image but more a feeling or an idea. It felt good and it felt right. So I started listening more, and when I listen, I always know what to do. The answers never come from others outside of me, but rather from deep inside me.

I can feel it in my body now too. There is a new sense of calm that's taken the place of tension, a faith in something divinely greater than myself. I also have a powerful faith in myself, and my own capacity to heal. As I take a well-needed 'soul sabbatical' from my coaching work, I am now having bursts of inspiration about my future direction and the unique way I would like to be of service in the world.

Finding stillness has been the most beneficial practice to reignite my passion.

We may act sophisticated and worldly but I believe we feel safest when we go inside ourselves and find home, *a place where we belong* and maybe the only place we really do.

- MAYA ANGELOU

LOVE IN ACTION

INNER PRACTICE
Connect With Your Knowing

We are all born with an in-built guidance system that we can consult at any time. It takes practice to hush the external noise and recognise your soul's unique way of communicating with you. Learning to trust your insight is a skill we can develop with practices. This guidance could come in a flash of inspiration, a picture, writing, synchronicities or deep bodily knowing. It presents differently for all of us. For me, I often connect most when I am doing activities that where I am running on automatic, like in the shower or driving on country roads or out in nature.

If you would like some guidance, try the following steps:

1. Remove yourself from outward distractions and find a quiet place
2. Get quiet within yourself
3. Breathe five (or more) deep breaths into your belly. Place your hand on your belly (womb) to be sure you are breathing this deeply.
4. Let any thoughts arising just float away.
5. Listen for your inner knowing, that quieter voice from within.
6. Trust in its guidance (this isn't always easy!)
7. Optional – Journal what has arisen for you.
8. Take action where appropriate.

OUTER PRACTICE
Asking for Guidance

Evoke for yourself the image of a higher power. They may or may not be in human form. Give it time and patience for it to show up and be aware of how it feels to be in the presence of this wisdom source. If you can, be humble and respectful of a source greater than yourself.

Ask for their guidance. Ask any question you want answered.

Listen and write what comes immediately. Trust what comes.

Am I open to considering cancer to be an opportunity for my soul to evolve?

If I knew that everything would work out beautifully, even better than I could hope for, how might I be experiencing my life right now?

How might I create more space in my life for quiet reflection to allow connection with the Divine?

How could I cultivate more receptivity for my guidance, inspiration and insights? What might I do with this information?

Stillness

PART 9

Accepting What Is

"Don't surrender your loneliness
So quickly.
Let it cut more deep.
Let it ferment and season you
As few human
Or even divine ingredients can.
Something missing in my heart tonight
Has made my eyes so soft
My voice
So tender,
My need of God
Absolutely
Clear."

- Hafiz

MINDFULNESS

The practice of mindfulness is being one with our present time experience, not consumed with thoughts and plans of the future or ruminating on the past but being right here, right now, in *this* moment.

For many of us, being present is challenging and difficult to achieve. Choosing not to disassociate from our experience but being right where we are and turning towards, rather than away from difficult emotional experiences is challenging, but a most helpful strategy during difficult times. I have always been future-focused and looking to what I could achieve next so the very thought of finding stillness in this moment felt counterintuitive.

In order for me to practice being mindful and do it even half well, I needed to let go of my tightly held grip on the reins of control and accept life's impermanence. One of life's greatest constants is its propensity to change. It's been said, 'life is not defined by the challenges we face but how we choose to respond to them'. Choosing to adapt and flex to meet each of life's changes have been tough lessons to learn.

The strategies practiced in mindfulness are designed to help us regulate our emotions, allowing us to live more fully in the present moment, regardless of what lies ahead. The inevitability of loss, change and eventual death are both more challenging and more amplified when met with a life threat like cancer.

Meeting cancer and accepting its arrival does not equate to 'giving up' or not trying to treat one's illness as proactively as we choose; rather, it acknowledges the reality of the situation and allows a turning away from blame and shame. Loss and grief are often inevitable emotions and shifting from blame towards acceptance may be more helpful.

CHAOS

I woke up today and felt inspired to meditate. I yearned to connect with a force greater than me and to feel myself more fully.

I kicked off my shoes and went outside to lie on the grass in my front yard. We are lucky to have a large, private yard with views as far as the eye can see. As I stretched out on the soft, lush grass I felt mother earth for the first time in a very long time. I wasn't sure if it was my anxiety or hers, but I felt panic. I felt trembling. And it was the strangest thing. I have always taken comfort that mother earth would be calm, supportive and always here to hold me but I didn't feel that today. Is she panicked? Is she angry? What is she feeling? *Or was it me?*

The Covid-19 pandemic has certainly grounded our country and totally changed our world. I am awe-struck that my cancer diagnosis and chemotherapy treatment are simultaneously occurring with this pandemic. I am feeling very rocked by this. I haven't watched any mainstream news about the virus and have actively chosen to refrain from having images of fear embedded into my psyche. However, I can FEEL this. It feels heavy. It is palpable.

Chaos often shows up when change is imminent. It's the uncomfortable, icky space I call the void, the Buddhists call the bardo, the state of the unknown between one stage and the next. This is the place we most often resist but if embraced and accepted allows the passage of transformation.

I have always been open and willing for change as I have seen this as an easier path than hanging onto the struggles and hurt. This isn't the chosen path for many, however. In my work, most people I encounter continue to tote around a big bag of worries and regrets from the past rather than risk the uncertainty of a life without them. Even if you could imagine a lighter, brighter future the subconscious patterns that keep us stuck are challenging to release.

In my experience, chaos is the perfect storm to shake up these patterns, and is always an opportunity to propel us forward.

Right now, I know I am in the biggest storm I have felt in this lifetime, and as much as there's a part of me who'd love to shrug it off as quickly as possible, I am equally excited about what this collective shift means for our world, politics, business, families and for me, personally.

I sense that I am on a new path and being guided to a new fate. I have always known I have a bigger purpose but have lacked the clarity to see it and hence forge ahead with it. *Am I being prepared for this now?*

Imagine for a moment, that this storm is preparing you for something bigger, something profound, something more. What might that something be?

FINDING MEANING

I learned somewhere along the way that I needed to strive to survive, that somehow who I was wasn't ever quite enough. If only I studied more, read more, worked harder, produced more then I would 'succeed', I would get ahead. In some perverse way my life would be worthwhile, or I might become worthy.

… Until I started asking myself what all the striving was truly for.

Where was I heading?
Who was I trying to impress?
What did I really want to achieve for myself if I stopped worrying what others thought?
How would I know when I'd done enough striving and had actually arrived at the utopian destination I was working so hard to get to?

In my early twenties I read a book that would change my outlook on life forever. 'Man's Search For Meaning' by Viktor Frankl was that book. Viktor was an Austrian psychiatrist and holocaust survivor. In his incredible book, he shares his unimaginable trials and tribulations as a prisoner in Nazi concentration camps. During his time at Auschwitz, Frankl came to believe that man's deepest desire is to search for meaning and purpose. He offers us all a way to transcend suffering and find significance in the art of living.

As I sat receiving my chemo infusions, I would ponder my plight as though breast cancer treatment was my own concentration camp of sorts. It certainly felt like it! Like Viktor, held captive in a place he didn't want to be, enduring the unimaginable, how could I too, see the bigger picture here and find purpose in all of this and how might it serve me in my life going forward? Could I perhaps be of support and benefit to others too? It was in these moments that the idea for this very Journal was born.

I know these are some seriously big questions to ask of oneself but in the midst of the darkest nights of my soul, questions of life and death, meaning and purpose were in the front of my mind.

For what purpose have I been given this experience? What good might come from all of this? How might I derive meaning and purpose from my experience of breast cancer?

EVICTION

I am in constant awe of life and how it is continually reflecting back that which I have yet to learn. So when our landlord informed us he was putting our home on the market, I could feel an inferno of feelings raging through my veins. I was in the midst of chemotherapy and isolating due to Covid-19 and all of a sudden we were having house inspections two and three times a week! My calm healing sanctuary was now a presentation home with dozens of strangers and potential risks coming through our home and we had no apparent control over the situation.

At first Chris and I got angry. How could the owners do this to us? How are they allowed to do this amidst Covid-19? But they were, and the house inspections continued. My blood boiled at the hard-nosed agent who had been appointed to sell the property and I railed against her complete lack of regard for our circumstances. Feeling powerless and furious was exhausting and draining and one day I decided that I was wasting far too much energy on a situation I couldn't change. I thought it better to invest my energy in figuring out where we wanted to go so we would be the ones giving notice before being evicted.

Surrendering to the situation at hand and shifting our focus to where we were heading led us to find the stunning white weatherboard house we now call home. In the blink of an eye, we organised a 30-day settlement and moved into our dream home within just a few short weeks. Life has a beautiful way of working out when we surrender to what is, rather than resisting.

RENOVATIONS

When we first inspected the house, we fell in love with it. We thought there were a few minor changes we would make but overall, the house was pretty close to perfect. We could move in straight away and get settled quickly. Given I was in the middle of this taxing treatment, this was our preferred option.

So when we invited a builder to give us a quote on upgrading the oven, this sparked a domino effect of changes in the kitchen as well as an extension involving the construction of a butler's pantry. Our visionary builder planted seeds of an even more beautiful space to call home and the renovations began. He suggested it might be a two-week project which I felt was an overly optimistic deadline to begin with but we got the job underway.

As I write we are now at 10-weeks from starting our butler's pantry. For seven weeks our only means of cooking was with an old electric frypan. We had no oven, stovetop, microwave and our fridge still sits on our back porch. I know these are classic 'first world' problems but it has been a true test of patience and surrender. During Covid-19 there have been plenty of supply chain issues and just about everyone has decided to renovate while they're stuck at home so getting tradesmen to come and do work has been exceptionally challenging.

My husband and I have had many a heated debate over this seemingly small renovation. My sense of urgency and the expectation of good customer service have been anything but helpful during this time. Deep breaths, more deep breaths. As I accept that this project has a timeline far different to the one I had in mind, rather than pushing and forcing, I am learning to let go and surrender to what is. Once again, life's gentle reminder that there is my plan and there is a greater plan, which I have little control over. I can kick and scream all I like but it won't make one iota of difference to getting these renovations done any quicker. In fact, it might be just the opposite.

Let go of the need to control
Trust in the process
Surrender to what is
More deep breaths.

Once again, I am reminded of the powerful lessons my life is showing me. Surrender is the key.

NON-STRIVING

In Buddhism, they speak of an attitude of 'non-striving'. To achieve inner peace one must let go of the need to be anywhere but in this moment, here and now. As a high achiever who once prided herself on productivity, the notion of non-striving felt so foreign it was incomprehensible. I've spent my entire life in pursuit of knowledge, relationships, jobs, status, money, rainbows. There was always another sparkly thing to pursue to keep me from sitting in the present moment and feeling what it is to be still. *What was I afraid of? What was I running from?* It's not as though it was a conscious decision I was making but more like a subconscious pattern that continued to play out, until I woke up to it.

Cancer treatment is definitely more of a slow burning marathon than a quick sprint. For most of my treatment, I wished I could just get it over with and get to the other side, striving for the day when it would all be done and I could get on with my life.

Sitting in stillness was the LAST thing I wanted to do. It was like the universe handed me the perfect storm to stop me dead in my tracks and force me to be still. As I had chosen to take time off work, I had far too many days to ponder my plight and get acquainted with the parts of me I had been running from.

I intuitively felt I was being held by a force, far greater than me. I called Her the Divine and I just knew She had my back.

Enduring a diagnosis and the associated treatment is just too much for one soul to handle. I knew I couldn't manage it on my own and out of sheer desperation, I began to pray. I prayed to this infinite, divine source that holds us all. I literally handed over my fears, my doubts, and my worries and admitted it was just too much for me to bear.

I did not have the capacity to carry this burden on my own and I was on my knees, pleading for help. I was like the bird clenching so tightly on to the branch, frozen with fear and unable to take flight. I felt as though I had no control, no certainty and no strength to manage what was happening. Confronted with my own mortality and enduring a marathon of treatments that made me feel sick, I was tired of the battle. Sooo. soooo t-i-r-e-d.

I instinctively threw up my hands and passed it all over to this divine, powerful and distinctly feminine force I could sense. The conversation went something like, 'Okay, I have nothing more to give. Do what you will with me. Have your way.' And just like that, I felt the sweet surrender. I trusted She would take me into Her arms and support me through this. I surrendered to the journey and I surrendered to being in the now.

There was nothing to pursue, nowhere more important I needed to be and nothing I could do to change the steps or the pace or the outcome of this experience. I was and always am in the perfect place, in this moment. Surrendering to what is and trusting in the unfolding. I released my tightly held grip on the reins of control and am now simply allowing the journey to evolve as it is intended.

My Dad used to call me his 'grass is greener girl', implying there's some place else I'd always rather be and noted I am perpetually focused on the future and believing that there is some place else that would be better than wherever I am. And he was right. My natural inclination is to keep moving, yes moving towards more and more of what I want to have in my life. *Is that such a bad thing? Wouldn't you?* It never occurred to me that in all this moving towards something, I was also always moving *away* from what IS, in the present moment.

I think a certain level of striving has served me well in many ways. I lead a pretty wonderful life as a result. What I've missed however, in all my striving is the journey itself. While I'm so busy in pursuit, I'm not taking time to smell the roses or spontaneously respond to joyful moments. For me, the goal was to get to the destination, as quickly as possible. It was never about enjoying the journey itself.

The irony too is that even our best-laid plans can be trumped and gazumped! I may attempt to over-control and over-engineer my life, but in the end, do we really ever have control? There always seems to be a higher power at play rendering our best laid plans into daydreams.

A bird sitting on a tree
is never afraid of the branch breaking,
because her trust is not on the branch
but on it's own wings.
Always believe in yourself.

– UNKNOWN.

Happiness,
not in another place
but this place...
not for another hour,
but this hour.

— WALT WHITMAN

What if the destination is actually the journey itself? What if there's actually nowhere to get to… that we've already arrived? I know that would make a massive difference to the way I live my life and my experience of it.

Stop striving,
Stop forcing,
Stop pushing.
Let go of control.
And just let things be.
S-u-r-r-e-n-d-e-r to the here and now.

ACCEPTANCE

I am well over the halfway mark in my treatment regime now. My chemo treatments are complete, my hair has regrown in all grey and curly (so unlike it was before) and my eyelashes are growing too, albeit painfully slowly. They are far from the thick, luscious lashes I once had and didn't truly appreciate until now. I'm also sporting an extra five kilos from when this journey began.

Even though I thought I was finished chemo, I can still feel the tingling in my fingers, a residual symptom of the drugs that once coursed through my body and I have the daily reminder I am still receiving Herceptin infusions as the plastic port in my chest sits uncomfortably like an irritating cockroach under my skin. I am to have Herceptin treatments for several more months and have scheduled a preventative bilateral mastectomy. Given my genetics it is probably wise to have the surgery but I'm not in any rush. I want to feel calm and prepared for this major surgery and ensure the appropriate time and space for healing.

Nearly a year from my diagnosis, I feel so tired from it all. I was exhausted before my diagnosis by life in general and the result of pushing to overcome so many hurdles, but I'm tired now in a new and different kind of way. Tired of the upheaval to my life, tired of treatments and the uncertainty of how my body will respond, tired of the waiting, full stop.

I have wanted so badly to race through all of this, to get to the other side as quickly as possible, to tick things off my treatment list. The truth of the matter is, however, there aren't any shortcuts through the outer circus of all these treatments or the inner journey of confronting my own mortality. I am smack dab in the middle of it all. The door to the life I once lived is firmly closed behind me, with no option to return, and the door to my future is becoming clearer like a developing polaroid picture but is still beyond my reach.

As the weeks and months pass, I feel my old habitual patterns of doing, doing, doing loosen their hold on me. There is no striving or racing or achieving to do now, no deadlines or rewards. I am still frustrated by this unsought change, and dreadfully miss the adrenaline pumped life I once lived and the sense of achievement I derived from working and achieving results.

As the shackles of my old ways fall away, I am getting acquainted with a new feeling emerging in its place. A sense of calm. An appreciation for the opportunity to take this quiet, peaceful, spacious time for me. A moment in my life where there is no place else to be but right here and now, in the present!

I do believe I have come to a place of acceptance. Acceptance of my diagnosis, acceptance of my journey, acceptance of life's ever-changing ways. I am right where I need to be.

SURRENDER

I can still feel the compulsion toward busy-ness and adrenaline rising up sometimes. Interestingly, my inner voice has also risen up and speaks so much more loudly now than these outer cultural impulses which have become faint, mere whispers. They no longer hold such relevance or importance in my life.

I have come to a place of complete surrender to all of it. Letting go of my need to control what will happen. I have little energy to resist what will be. I find I am at my strongest when I'm able to let go. When I suspend my thoughts and beliefs I then leave myself open to all possibilities. It just so happens that this is when I'm able to experience the most clarity and wisdom too. I now see my need for certainty was actually blocking me from having greater awareness.

I have given up any desire to race through it all. Instead, I want to meet this experience face to face and to learn from it, to become better for it.

I find myself moving further inward now. A part of me wants to just skip back into life as though all of this was a bad dream but another part of me feels drawn to the yet unknown parts of this experience, into deeper aspects of myself to meet myself *all the way down* to the core.

Serenity Prayer

God, grant me the serenity
to accept the things I cannot change,
the courage to change the things I can,
and the wisdom to know the difference.

– REINHOLD NIEBUHR

When the voice and the vision on the inside
becomes louder and more profound
than the voice and the vision on the outside,
you have begun to master your life.

- DR JOHN DEMARTINI

The masks that once gave me so much comfort and protection from the world no longer fit me or meet my needs. I seem to be more sensitive and aware and less tolerant of the games people play and cringe at the habitual insincerity. It has become increasingly difficult for me to engage in conversations about everyday events. My attention span has become shorter and I have completely lost interest in what is going on in the world of politics and news, and sometimes even find it hard to engage with news of what friends are up to around me. Yet, I find myself mesmerised by the blossoming of a flower, the colours of the sky as the sun sets or the feeling of the water washing over my feet as I walk along the beach. It is as though I am experiencing the beauty of the world's simplicity for the first time.

I no longer have the need for a wide network of friends, choosing instead to have fewer, yet quality people in my life. Cancer's presence has initiated an evaluation of what and who are important in my life and where I choose to spend my precious days.

The 'go-getter' in me has retired and in her place is a new woman who yearns for quiet, calm spaciousness. I have spent so much of my life trying to please others, to fit in, to do the right things in the hope of being deemed worthy and lovable. Somehow the thoughts and opinions of others matter less to me now. What matters is what I think of me. I am reclaiming my own authority and giving value to what I have to say.

As I continue diving deeper into my experience of treatment and of life more broadly, it feels as though I have a new level of awareness and objectivity. I see my life as a rich tapestry being intricately woven, each thread from the past an important part of who I've become. I have gratitude for each and every person that has come into my life, even those where there has been hurt for they have played their part in shaping who I am, now.

Most importantly, I feel happier in my own company and feel a renewed sense of passion for my creativity, my work and interests, my loved ones, the rhythm and cycles of nature and life itself. Rather than merely being alive, I now FEEL alive. It's as though I have woken from a deep slumber and view my world in merry wonderment for all of it's wacky and magical ways.

LOVE IN ACTION

INNER PRACTICE
Non-striving

Whenever possible, deliberately create some space to do nothing. You may want a timer for this practice. Start with 5-10 minutes and build on this.

Give yourself time to just 'be'; be free from any agenda, goal or effort. There is no desired outcome other than the experience of non-doing and non-striving.

Notice what happens without the habitual momentum of efforting.

We are human 'beings', not human 'doings'.

OUTER PRACTICE
Letting Go

To fully accept where we are now can often involve a conscious letting go of some aspects of ourselves.

Very often clinging to the past is what keeps us from accepting the truth of the present.

Take the time to craft your own ritual to honour and let go of those aspects that are no longer appropriate to this stage of your life. This will often be a tender process of grieving and can also be very freeing and an empowering part of your journey.

In my experience, I chose to let go of past relationships, my old professional persona, my old body image and looks. I felt I needed to explore and renegotiate various old contracts that no longer served me, whether they were spoken or unspoken.

Allow your creativity to flow in the many ways you may craft your ritual(s) to acknowledge this powerful, grieving practice. Some gentle suggestions to symbolise releasing of the past could include: clearing collections of old belongings, burning, burying, releasing into the wind, having conversations, writing letters, smudging and casting into the ocean to complete unfinished business.

What might you do for yourself to accomplish this?

Imagine if I were to surrender my suffering to the Divine or a higher power... what might be different for me?

Who am I becoming?

What's changed?
What's always been true about me?

What do I love and value about myself?

What's in the way of me fully accepting my reality now?

How does it feel in my body to fully and lovingly accept my current circumstances?

Summer

PART 10

My Wisest Healer

"Heal yourself with the light of the sun and the rays of the moon.
With the sound of the river and the waterfall.
With the swaying of the sea and the fluttering of birds.
Heal yourself with mint, neem, and eucalyptus.
Sweeten with lavender, rosemary, and chamomile.
Hug yourself with the cocoa bean and a hint of cinnamon.
Put love in tea instead of sugar and drink it looking at the stars.
Heal yourself with the kisses that the wind gives you
and the hugs of the rain.
Stand strong with your bare feet on the ground
and with everything that comes from it.
Be smarter every day by listening to your intuition,
looking at the world with your forehead.
Jump, dance, sing, so that you live happier.
Heal yourself, with beautiful love, and always remember ...
you are the medicine."

- María Sabina, Mexican healer and poet

BODY INTELLIGENCE

The wise healer within is your body's best barometer and always knows just what your body needs. I call this capacity your inner knowing or your intuition. Unfortunately, many of us have disconnected from the wisdom of our inner knowing. Often in subconscious protection of old hurts and trauma, habits develop so we 'numb out' with alcohol, drugs, sex, caffeine rather than feel the full spectrum of emotions that carry this wisdom.

When we dissociate from our body, we don't hear the whispers it is communicating as a call for our need for care. Our bodies are a brilliant gateway to our intuition when we learn to respect and listen to their wisdom.

INNOCENCE

One evening my friend Benay, and her young daughter, Mya came to visit us for a campfire out under a wondrous sky of shimmering stars. One of my favourite places in the world is to sit out under the night sky with the warmth of a campfire at our feet and the smell of roasting marshmallows. We sat mesmerised by the hypnotic flames when Mya blurted out of nowhere, 'How did you get cancer"? Caught off guard, I replied, "I don't know".

Mya continued on chatting about other things but her innocent question sent a wave of inquiry pinging around inside my mind and body like a ball in a pinball machine. Her question sent me to places I hadn't been before, busily and determinedly searching for an answer. *Where did my cancer come from? And why was it here?*

OPTIMAL HEALTH

I had already started reading the book, *Mind over Medicine* by Dr Lissa Rankin. Lissa is a GP and the daughter of a doctor. She was brought up in the traditional ways of western medicine until she woke up to the realisation that these traditional methods weren't really working for her or her patients.

She started noticing that some people were coming to her who appeared healthy on the surface and yet their bodies told a different story. They were eating super healthily, were very active and fit, looked amazing but were actually very unwell. So she started asking them some different questions. Questions I have never been asked by any doctor I've been to.

She asked things like:
- *Is anything keeping you from being the most authentic, vital you?*
- *What do you love and celebrate about yourself?*
- *What's missing from your life?*
- *Are you in a romantic relationship? Are you happy there?*
- *Are you fulfilled at work?*
- *Are you in touch with your life purpose?*
- *Do you express yourself creatively?*
- *Do you have a relationship to a higher power?*
- *Do you have a spiritual practice?*

It is a brilliant book and one that has changed my outlook forever. Dr Rankin discovered through her research and clinical work with patients, that the most significant contributing factor for optimal health is … are you ready for it? Yes, happiness.

I'd like to think that if doctors were asking us these quality questions and encouraging us to live in closer alignment to what brings us joy, fewer of us would be living with undiagnosed illness, or medicating our lives away.

What if it is as simple as that? What if finding more ways to bring joy and happiness into my life is the best treatment?

ROOT CAUSE

After years of working with her patients and applying her methodology to her own life, Dr Rankin began to see that it wasn't our doctors that had the power to heal us, rather it is our own mind that has that power. We truly have the power to heal ourselves.

As you can imagine, her work took on a new focus in her desire to empower and enable her patients to be their own best and wisest healer. It's a courageous and lofty invitation from a medical doctor. She began to get curious about not just their presenting symptoms, but their lifestyle, relationships and happiness too.

She saw herself more as a coach, guiding her patients to explore various aspects of their lives that just might hold the key to their health and wellbeing.

Two of her exploratory questions which I found most profound are:

What do you think might lie at the root of your illness?
And, what does your body need to heal?

The point is that
health is not static;
it is normal to lose it periodically
in order to come back to it
in a better way.

- ANDREW WEIL M.D.

In the midst of winter,
I found there was an
invincible summer.

- ALBERT CAMUS

As a professional coach, I get excited about the power of quality questions like these and their ability to initiate a healing response, merely by inquiring within oneself.

OMG! I knew the answers in the blink of an eye. I could feel myself sinking into my chair as I uttered the words out loud, *'I just need to rest'.* I am so emotionally, spiritually and physically tired. My soul is exhausted. I am depleted and have nothing left in reserve from giving, giving, giving. Putting on a brave and smiley face when all I really wanted to do was curl up and sleep. Whoa! What a powerful yet truthful expression of how I honestly felt.

A wave of gratitude washed over me as I realised that I have been gifted the perfect opportunity to rest. With the world in shutdown over the Covid-19 pandemic, my wedding celebrations all cancelled and squared away and fourteen months of chemo and Herceptin treatments ahead, I had literally NOTHING else to do but rest. Wow, did I actually manifest this or is someone upstairs truly looking out for me and making sure I get a break? I mean a real cortisol reducing, parasympathetic nervous system reboot that my body so desperately needed.

HEALING INSIDE-OUT

At the age of 49, my life felt more like I'd been put through the ringer cycle of a washing machine than my vision to be basking in the full blossoming of my well-tended garden by now!

I had moved my life overseas, catapulting myself thousands of miles from friends, family and everything familiar. I moved to Australia to marry a man who I believed was my knight in shining armour and the love of my life. Yes, I have read one too many fairy tales! Unfortunately, he didn't feel the same way and exited my life abruptly, ripping my heart out as he left. I was left to pick up the pieces of a life I wasn't truly happy in if I was honest with myself and build a new life with my three year-old son Josh. I found myself living in a tiny little town with zero career options, so I started a business to make ends meet. I have been fortunate to juggle running a business with being a pretty good Mom but the responsibility and constant financial worry took their toll.

Lost and lonely, I attracted a few 'bad-for-me' men who would suck any remaining bits of my heart and soul and depleted the final dregs of energy I had left. When I finally dragged up enough courage to boot the last energy vampire to the curb, I felt like I'd survived a tornado and was left with a pile of debris to sort through and re-build.

With my stress response in overdrive, it's no surprise my physical and emotional wellbeing took a downhill slide. This was around the time that breast cancer showed up the first time. I was constantly exhausted, riddled with pain and inflammation throughout my body. I couldn't sleep long enough to restore my energy and vitality and there was little joy or any real presence in my days. I felt dull and listless as I endeavoured to function as a business owner and a Mom. I was barely coping, making it through my days on autopilot.

For the past few years, the coach in me started to build a picture of what I wanted to make of my life, to get clear on the things I wanted to have more of so I could enjoy my life rather than just endure it. I wanted to have a loving relationship with a man, build a stronger relationship with my son, re-shape my business to be more aligned with my passions and strengths and I wanted to enjoy better physical fitness.

What I didn't realise was that my vision for a better and more beautiful life came from an intellectual, head space rather than a heart space. I was *'thinking'* this vision but was unable to *'feel'* it. Instead, all I could feel was the sheer weight of responsibility and a sense of being compelled to meet the pressures imposed by others.

Living with a rising undercurrent of bitterness and regret, I trundled through my days wondering if there would ever be time for me - time to just stop, breathe and smile. Despite the arrival of Chris, a beautiful soul who has since become my husband, I had not yet found true inner peace and balance in my life. It was around this time that my second breast cancer diagnosis arrived, with a much more aggressive message this time, one that I could not avoid.

The beauty of time is that it allows the heart and soul to mend as we slowly start to make sense and find perspective on the events that make up our life. The truth was there was a silver lining in all this. There always is. The multiple mini-crises I have endured have all contributed to what I call 'my awakening'. Each mini-crisis chipped another crack in the armour I had been wearing to fit in and to survive and prepared me for what needed to be altered radically for my soul healing to begin.

When breast cancer showed up the second time, this seismic crack ripped through me like only a life-threatening diagnosis could. It was during this whirlwind that I came to discover a long-lost part of myself. We all have this part within us. It's the radiant, life force at your centre – you may call it your Highest Self, your Christ Consciousness, your Buddha Nature, or what I call your soul. It's that part of you that's divine, whole, authentic and inextinguishable. Do you remember her? Have you ever met her?

And the day came
when the risk to remain tight in a bud
was more painful than
the risk it took to *blossom*.

- ANAIS NIN

Meditate for an hour every day,
unless you are too busy.
In that case meditate for two hours.

— ZEN PROVERB

During the depths of my cancer treatment, I found within myself a kind of wisdom, a sense of knowing that gradually began to take the helm. Amidst the fatigue and nausea of my chemo treatments, I experienced an awakening, a homecoming, finally returning to really inhabit my body after all of those years of being checked-out.

My friend Leonie says our body communicates with us all the time. She believes our body starts with a 'whisper', then a 'tap' and then a 'slap'. Whatever it takes until we actually hear and heed its message.

My body has been whispering to me for over a decade, more like two decades, but I had been ignoring it. So, in order to get my attention, the messages progressed to a tap and then a full-on slap. A breast cancer diagnosis was the perfect way to get my attention and bring me to my knees. I had no choice but to listen then!

I started listening to my body and my inner knowing and began to connect with myself in ways that were new to me. I started realising and understanding things about myself I hadn't noticed before. It became clear what might have caused my breast cancer to return and what needed to change in my life to help me heal and return to optimal health.

Facing the changes I knew I needed to make filled me with excitement. That may sound crazy, but I took my healing journey on as a special project. I gave it a flashy name 'My Soul's Sabbatical', carved out the time to commit to treatments and rest and surrounded myself with several wise and compassionate souls to support me through this journey.

TAKING A LEAP

My current life was no longer sustainable. I wasn't truly happy there anyway. I was tired of living my life by others' rules and expectations and as the habit of people-pleasing became increasingly unbearable, the frustration and disappointment in my life was impossible to ignore. One of my coach mentors once said that when the pain of staying where you are exceeds the fear of the unknown, you take a leap of faith. You do what it takes.

My friends kept telling me I was so brave. However, I didn't see it that way. The pragmatist in me saw that I had two real choices; the first, to retreat and deny what was happening and the second, to embrace my circumstances and look to expand and grow from them. It was like asking, 'will you choose to flounder or flourish from this?' I will choose to flourish every time.

MY DIAGNOSIS

Once I managed to get over the initial shock and overwhelm of my diagnosis and the reality of my projected year and a half of treatment ahead, I empowered my own wisest healer to connect with the magnitude of my current situation and inquire further into what sat at the very core of this disease residing in my body.

I knew I was exhausted. I had been running on empty longer than I cared to remember. Although I have enjoyed good health, or rather, the absence of illness, most of my life, I have spent thousands of dollars going to healers, masseurs, acupuncturists, dieticians, therapists and clairvoyants in pursuit of feeling vibrant and energetic. I knew there was more than the lethargic, adrenal-fatigued version of me I had grown to accept as my normal self.

I have endured a number of significantly stressful events in my life, each a trauma in their own way. Some massive, life-changing ones and some smaller, more bearable ones and yet each of them triggered a stress response that went ignored and got overridden. Without an appropriate release of these traumas, and the time to integrate and return to balance, the effect in my body had become compounded and the consequences acute.

Having awareness of my exhaustion was the first layer of the onion but I wanted to unpack what sat right at the root of this disease. *What was the cause of these cancer cells appearing? Just as important, what did I need to do to heal?*

WRITE YOUR REMEDY

While it's most likely too late to prevent this disease if it has already affected you, it's never too late to reduce the stresses in your life and create more opportunity for relaxation and healing. Imagine if you could mobilise your body's natural mechanisms of self-repair just by introducing actions and activities that bring you more joy, happiness and calm. That sounds like a perfect pathway to health in my books!

Your inner knowing is your best guide. Always. Your medical team has likely already set in motion a series of treatments to assist in returning you to optimal health on a physical level. I took great comfort however, in believing that I had some control and influence in achieving my own vibrant health. I chose to develop my own plan of complementary treatments to address the emotional, psychological and spiritual aspects of my healing to work in tandem with traditional clinical methods.

LOVE IN ACTION

INNER PRACTICE
What Does My Body Need?

We are far more intelligent than we know. What if we already knew what our diagnosis was before the doctor does?

Right here. This moment. Breathe in deeply. Exhale slowly. Feel into your body. Your head, your heart, your stomach, your lungs. Your root, your base, your spine. Feel deep into your solar plexus, right there in the centre of your chest.

What does your body need to heal? Tune in to your body, your heart, your life force. Go beyond the prescriptions set by your doctor. Listen. Listen intently. Dig deeper than any story you've been told. You may hear the faintest whisper. Or the loudest bellow. Go beyond the limits of your history. Listen for her. She is trying to reach you. Right here. This moment. What do you need right now?

Tune into your body now and ask your infinite wisdom what may be your diagnosis?

OUTER PRACTICE
My Healing Remedy

In order to heal my body, mind and soul, I first identified the needs and imbalances that I sensed in my body and my life and then considered what ingredients or actions I could take that would most support and enable my healing process.

MY NEEDS, PROMPTS, IMBALANCES	MY HEALING INGREDIENTS + ACTIONS
I believe breast cancer has visited me a second time and has an important message for me and my soul's evolution. I don't feel I have enough spiritual knowledge currently.	Seek out great spiritual teachers who may offer insights and guidance to more peacefully navigate my journey and glean the lessons I am here to receive.
I can't get through my healing journey on my own. I need the help, support and compassion of others.	Enlist the support of a varied group of spiritual teachers, naturopaths, wise women, friends, therapists and caring souls to complement the work of my medical team.
I feel disconnected from my body and generally feel quite numb in my life. I want to feel more fully and receive the messages from my body before it's too late.	- Do activities that bring me into my body and make me feel happy. - Meditate daily - Dance often - Enjoy wonderful love-making - Take warm baths - Take regular beach or forest walks
I feel disconnected from my family. They are thousands of miles from me. I want to feel more connected despite the distance between us.	Facetime my parents and sisters more regularly.
I don't feel loving kindness and compassion from my family.	Give them and myself what I most wish to receive.
I lack clarity of my life's purpose anymore. I yearn for more clarity and insight about my future direction.	Get quiet. Breathe. Listen more. Allow my purpose to show up.
I feel thwarted creatively. I haven't assigned any value to creativity in my life but feel this is a critical part of my healing process.	- Get painting - Journal more often - Bake beautiful cakes

Explore what practices are right to pursue for your body.
Create your own healing remedy in the space provided below.

MY NEEDS, PROMPTS, IMBALANCES	MY HEALING INGREDIENTS + ACTIONS

MY NEEDS, PROMPTS, IMBALANCES	MY HEALING INGREDIENTS + ACTIONS
I yearn to have a stronger Divine connection but the religion I grew up in is not the right model for me.	- Create an altar at home - Pray daily - Spend time tending my personal altar
I long to let go of the many masks I wear and be truly seen and appreciated for who I am.	Commit to discarding my masks and be unapologetically me in all areas of my life.
I'm not clinically depressed and tend to be a happy and cheerful person much of the time, but there's a deep underlying sadness within me. I'd like to explore and heal my sadness so I can experience more joy.	- Journal more - Practice giving thanks everyday and jot them down in a special diary
I keep a frenetic pace and would like to slow down, giving space between activities to allow for more joy.	- Set an intention each day to achieve just three things - Take pause and drink tea throughout the day - Laugh more
I don't feel my home environment is conducive to my healing and would like to create a healing space that is relaxing and nourishing for my soul.	Have a feng shui consultant assess our home Create a healing home environment complete with candles, plants/flowers, essential oils, cashmere lap blanket, beautiful journal and pens and healthy nourishing foods and friends that lift me up
I feel as though I've lived much of my life feeling numb and disassociated from myself and others. I want to be more aware and grateful for the big as well as the small things in my life.	Express daily gratitudes. I love the practice of giving thanks for the beautiful things no matter how big or small that show up in my life. I keep a beautiful diary on my bedside table and love to write down what I'm grateful for before I go to sleep.
I worry about all of the chemicals that are prevalent in my modern day life. Whether it's using deodorant, skin care, make-up, the foods I eat, toxic cleaning products and chemicals used in my garden.	I aim to live a more chemical free life by changing up the products I use daily. I no longer use regular deodorants and have opted for a natural one. I will only use natural skin care and make-up products, vinegar and baking soda for cleaning products.

Explore what practices are right to pursue for your body.
Create your own healing remedy in the space provided below.

MY NEEDS, PROMPTS, IMBALANCES	MY HEALING INGREDIENTS + ACTIONS

What do I believe may be at the root of my illness?

If I truly am my own wisest healer, what do I know I most need to do in order to restore balance?

What are the specific ingredients in the remedy for my healing?

If my cancer had a message for me, what might it have to say?

What brings me joy and happiness right now?
How can I cultivate more joy and happiness?

What rules do I follow in my life that I wish I could break?

What are you grateful for in your life?
Write down anything that comes to mind, even the smallest of things.

Serenity

PART 11

Living My Soulful Life

"I believe that the soul is the essence of who and what we are. It comes with codes and possibilities and the next layers of who and what we may yet be. It is often a pain in the neck because it says wake up, it's time to wake up, don't go to sleep. I think it is also the lure of our becoming."

- Jean Houston

NIRVANA

One of the most powerful discoveries in this walk through cancer, is the remembrance that there is, and always has been, a life meant for me that is truer and more soul-aligned than the one I've been living.

However in order to manifest it, I needed to be able to picture it for myself, feel myself really occupying life during and beyond cancer. Only I can imagine that better way of being and only I can manifest it. I discovered I truly am a powerful creator!

The better life is what Jews call shalom, Buddhists call nirvana, Christians call heaven, Muslims call salaam, and many agnostics call peace.

On earth as it is in heaven.

Going through treatment for breast cancer has been a rollercoaster ride in many ways. It has been a true test of patience, and for someone like me who has little patience at all and just wants to get on with things, this long haul of appointments, uncertainty and lack of control has been excruciating at times.

My normal modus operandi is to keep busy, enjoy lots of variety, distract myself regularly so I rarely find the time or space or the desire, frankly, to sit in quiet contemplation. Until now, I viewed 'quiet' as synonymous with boredom. I have never learned how to relate to myself or enjoy my own company for long and have always preferred the company of others to the nonsense that percolates in my head.

So for many days and weeks throughout treatment, I have been bored out of my mind; nowhere to go, nothing to do, no distractions to divert my attention from me.

In such moments, life's deeper, more profound questions began to arise. *What do I want to do with this life? What's important to me? What do I want to let go of? How do I want to be remembered?*

It's often the moment when the discomfort of sitting in the unknown becomes too much, when we don't know how to proceed, that in the very next moment we find ourselves. Right after prickly boredom comes self-discovery. We do, however, have to hang in there long enough without jumping ship to avoid discomfort. What I found is that cancer treatment offers the perfect cocktail of sheer frustration and boredom with no escape route possible. You are on this journey whether you like it or not.

There were many days I was sure I had hit rock bottom, but instead of seeing it as an ending, I chose to see it as the beginning of something beautiful and new.

Between every thought there is a little space.
That still presence that you feel, that's your soul.

And if you get really in touch with it,
if you become familiar with this centre of awareness
that you really are,
you will see it's your ticket to freedom.

- DEEPAK CHOPRA

SOUL'S TRUTH

I have never been one to sit and stew in painful situations or emotions, preferring to be more future-focussed and solve the 'problem' with action. I guess in many ways the eternal optimist in me chose to see what's possible and make lemonade when life served me lemons. So in many ways, designing my preferred future landscape is something I have been perfecting for years. Now, many months out of chemotherapy and a few months away from a bilateral mastectomy, my excitement and enthusiasm for designing my beautiful new soul-led life is mixed with fear and a little resistance.

The person I once was has morphed and changed into the person I'm becoming. The rules, expectations and ways of living that once gave me certainty and comfort no longer hold true for me. The need for outer approval holds little value. What interests me most is my soul's longing. My soul's truth. What does she most desire? What is her ultimate vision?

Have I stepped into my sovereignty? Have I finally connected with my own power rather than giving it away to others? Is this what it feels like when the voice on the inside is louder than those on the outside?

I'm not sure exactly when it happened but I noticed I've become enchanted with the voice of my own inner wisdom. I've come to see that no one outside of me truly knows who I am or can know what I need to do to heal or to grow. Experts, ministers, therapists, authors, family and friends may offer their best advice, but even those who love me the most can never really know what's right for me. No one else is just like me with the challenges and gifts and history I have. I am the best possible navigator seeking and exploring this uncharted territory.

We all are.

Your Soul's Truth

Trust that you know.
How you really feel.
What you really see.
What you know to be true.
Who you are in your soul.
Beneath your doubts and rumination and endless
questions, there is an ocean of silent knowing.

That right there: that's your soul's truth.
Your soul arrived already knowing what to do,
how to be, what the answers are.
Stop questioning yourself.
Trust it.

- MEGAN DALLA-CAMINA

DELIBERATE DESIGN

One sad and lonely day during treatment I had the crazy idea that instead of feeling sorry for myself, I could set out to start visioning how I wanted to experience my life during and after treatment.

If you can dream it, you can do it. - Walt Disney

I began to list the things that were important to me and I wrote them using language as though I was already living them.

This is what I came up with:

- My body is healthy and vital and strong
- I mindfully and calmly navigate my treatment and my life
- I trust in my treatment plan and that I'm where I need to be
- I have great breasts (reconstructed) at the end
- I have clarity of my soul's purpose and how I can best be of service
- I have gained the insights and wisdom for optimal health and zero cancer recurrence
- I feel, enjoy, experience and love my life fully
- I have immense gratitude for everything
- I have fully re-charged my energetic batteries and naturally live a more attuned life
- I have a loving relationship with my beloved, Chris
- I am resolving my family wounds and have made peace with my family

What would you like to make manifest in your life during treatment and beyond?

3 STEPS TO...
Manifesting What I Want

I am blessed to have a group of women in my life I call my soul sisters. We have been catching up each week via zoom. During one of our many discussions we talked about how we could best go about manifesting what we want. These women are some of the wisest, most connected souls I know, so when we co-create ideas I get pretty excited. We came up with these three steps to manifesting.

The first and third step are super obvious and already a well-worn path for this high achiever. However, step two was a step that I had never considered or tried before but it made perfect sense and I was excited to give it a try.

Step 1 - *Setting my intention*

What is it I most want to manifest? What will it look like and what it will feel like? And how will I know I've achieved it?

Eg. Chris and I are looking to buy a new home. We know the general area we want to live in and ideally want a house with a view of nature and a swimming pool.

Step 2 - *Surrender to my intention*

Become still and quiet, breathe, rest, take some time to get clear before hopping straight into the action step. Allow my intention to become clearer. Be open to the mystery. Broaden my vision. Look for coincidences. Receive any insights, messages and dreams to help create a clearer vision of my intention. Really feel into this step. Allow the details of the vision to come to me.

Eg. Once we had set our intention, the picture of our dream home became clearer and clearer. We wanted four bedrooms, a pool, a natural treed setting, an indoor/outdoor feel, loads of natural light, inspiring kitchen and so on.

Step 3 - *Take expansive action*

Once I've allowed enough time (I will have a sense), and my intention is clear, it's time to take action. I can wish all I want, but action is surely necessary for me to achieve my goals.

Eg. Equipped with a list of criteria about our dream home, Chris and I began our search for a house that felt right. Knowing the aspects that made up our dream home, we were able to find it in a few short weeks.

LOVE IN ACTION

INNER PRACTICE

Commitments to Your Soul

What are your daily commitments to your soul?

It could be your meditation practice, keeping your word to yourself and others, creating loving boundaries, building a personal altar or small daily rituals that keep you tuned in and on your path.

Write down your daily commitments here.

OUTER PRACTICE
Creating a Vision Board

One of the most valuable practices I do every year is start by envisioning the type of year ahead that I would most desire. What would make this the most amazing year of my life? Who do I want to have in my life? What work and activities do I want to do more of? How could I enjoy this year even more?

I collect old magazines and pictures throughout the year so that when I get to this creating phase I have plenty of images to work with.

Purchase some poster board the size you would like your final Vision Board to be.

Grab your scissors and glue-stick, put on some fun music and get busy creating a vision board of the life you would most like to live. If you're good at drawing, you can draw images too. Add stickers and glitter. Get creative and have fun with this project.

I hang mine on my office wall so that I am continually reminded as to what is important to me. I am amazed at the end of each year just how much of my vision has actually come true. After all, we are power manifestors! So investing a little bit of time to get clear on what we want more of is a sure way of living a wonderfully beautiful life.

Envision

How could I be more deeply attuned to my inner wisdom?

What makes me feel spiritually connected?

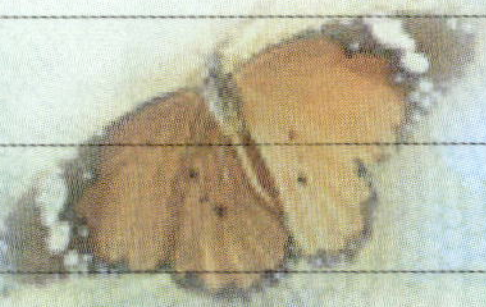

What is it I most desire to be, do or have?

In what ways if any, is fear holding me back from realising my dreams?

If I was a powerful manifestor, I would create...
What are some specific steps I could take right now to manifest this?

How might this be of benefit to you?
How might this be of benefit to others?

How do I feel living the full expression of my most beautiful life?

Peace

PART 12

Love of My Life

TODAY

"Today I'm flying low and I'm not saying a word.
I'm letting all the voodoos of ambition sleep.

The world goes on as it must,
the bees in the garden rumbling a little,
the fish leaping, the gnats getting eaten.
And so forth.

But I'm taking the day off. Quiet as a feather.
I hardly move though really I'm travelling a terrific distance

Stillness. One of the doors into the temple."

- Mary Oliver

FITTING IN

I've spent my whole life feeling like I'm not enough or I'm too much or that I'm different and I don't belong. I've literally spent years trying to contort myself into what I thought others wanted me to be. I made others' behaviour mean something about me. I believed that in some way something I said or did caused 'them' to treat me that way, and that I must have deserved it.

I moved to Australia when I was twenty-five years old, so full of excitement and hope to build a new life with my husband, at the time. From the wintery cold of Canada, Australia seemed like my promised land. I felt as though the utopia of bright sunshine and sandy beaches I had seen in the poster on my bedroom wall as a child had truly come to life.

However, as I settled into the new culture, the subtle differences to the life I had known before became increasingly apparent. People were different. The way people interacted and spoke was different. Yet again, I felt I didn't fit in and my distorted self-belief that I was a misfit and I didn't belong anywhere was further reinforced.

As a coping strategy I donned a cloak of disguise to appear less intense, less intelligent, less opinionated; I became a mere shadow of my former self. I spent years trying to be 'beige' so as not to stand out, offend or be rejected. I had lost my colour and sparkle. It took so much energy to wear this cloak and these masks to conceal my true nature.

What I found was that playing small not only exhausted me, it actually blocked genuine connection with others. I wasn't risking putting my true self out there and not surprisingly, people were connecting with my masks rather than my true essence, the real me. Professor and author, Brené Brown once said, 'the number one barrier to belonging is fitting in.' It's a guaranteed formula for loneliness. Stripping off our masks and letting our true radiance shine fully may not be comfortable but is the best way to allow for deeper connection. It takes real courage to be unapologetically yourself.

I've always craved deeper connections and conversations, which is probably why the profession of coaching was so appealing. But who was I being as a coach, mother, lover and friend if I couldn't be myself? I was not living the full expression of myself, just a diluted version of who I really am.

UNAPOLOGETICALLY ME

Going through treatment and losing my hair felt like the old me was washing away like my hair down the drain. In its place a new sense of self was emerging. I was re-discovering forgotten parts of myself that had been buried under mountains of debris, collected over years. All the masks fell away. They no longer fit the no-fuss person I was becoming.

In a way, finishing chemo has been my re-birth. Watching my hair re-grow in shades of curly grey and white, is completely different from the hair I'd known. As I look in the mirror, someone different looks back at me now and it's not just the change of hair colour. She has the same deep green eyes but someone new is looking through them. There's a strong, vibrant, colourful woman, deeply connected with what's true on the inside with little concern for what others think of her.

Such freedom, such release to let go of the old strategies and be truly seen for who I am, in all my brilliance, and to be unapologetically the full expression of me.

What if cancer came to visit me not to scare me to death but to scare me into life? Was I actually really living before my diagnosis? … or merely meandering through life? Was I too busy trying to fit in and impress others? Whose life was I really living?

CINDY-RELLA

As a young girl, I grew up with fairy tales like Cinderella. Like so many others, Cinderella is a classic folk tale teaching young minds that love is something you seek outside of yourself rather than something that already exists within you. We are led to believe that a prince on a white horse will come and rescue us and complete our living fairy tale.

I used to love these stories and read them over and over. I'm pretty sure this is where my desire to have a strong, handsome, supportive man in my life came from and how I came to create my own Cindy-rella story. I used to believe that I wasn't loveable unless I had a man whose constant presence proved to me that I was worthy of being loved. Once upon a time, I used to think that my life, my career, all my worldly success meant nothing unless I had a man by my side. Subconsciously I believed that love started from a place outside of me and I had to wait for another person to shower me with love before I could love myself.

As my friend Bart says, our first love affair is the one we have with ourselves. Only then can we be a beacon of love and genuinely give and receive love from others. Having love for oneself first is the foundation for all love. It is our soul's truth.

*Close your eyes and fall in love.
Stay there.*

— RUMI

LOVE CURES

Living in alignment with our soul's truth, is one of the most challenging yet rewarding paths to happiness. True happiness begins with genuine self-love and acceptance of our humanity, in all our imperfections. Only then can we truly love others with sincerity and compassion.

You've heard that right: love cures all, much more literally than modern medicine would have you believe. This is how the body, mind and soul connection works, the idea of the whole-body incarnate.

As Chopra and Tanzi write:

'Humans live for meaning and the personal value of every experience. The body metabolises our experiences and sends the message to every cell, while the mind, in its own domain, processes experiences in terms of sensations, images, thoughts, and feelings. Nothing fuses the healing effects of the whole-system like the love of the human heart.'

GRATITUDE

Having love in your heart and an attitude of gratitude is the pathway to heaven on earth. It is how we connect and align with the Divine all around us and within us.

When stress and anxiety show up and we are feeling disconnected from ourselves and others the best antidote is to give thanks. Choosing to focus on what we have to be grateful for shifts our attention from what we *have not*. Clearing energy and feelings of lack that stem from fear creates opportunity and space to be lovingly reminded of all there is to be abundantly thankful for.

My mother always said, 'be sure to say thank you' for what you receive. I feel a deep sense of gratitude for the good, bad and the ugly. ALL of it has brought me to here and now.

May I live my life as a never-ending prayer of gratitude for having finally brought me home to myself. And most importantly, my gratitude to the Divine for awakening me to the strength, love and wisdom within me.

One day, a light will go off.

You'll see yourself as you really are.
You'll stop seeking validation.
The opinions of others will no longer matter.
You will see how far you've come
and feel your own strength.
Then, you smile.
You smile because
you are in the presence of greatness.

- SAMANTHA MOULTRUP

METAMORPHOSIS

I'm still on my treatment journey, having Herceptin treatments and awaiting a double mastectomy later in the year, but already my metamorphosis is in progress. I can feel it in my body. Like the butterfly breaking free of her chrysalis, I too feel the cocoon of my own making is unravelling. I have outgrown it in many ways and couldn't fit back into it even if I tried.

What if I am already perfectly perfect in my imperfections? What if I am enough, already? And I have nothing I need to strive for, achieve in order to be loved?

As sung by the former Cat Stevens, Yusuf Islam,
'To be what you must, you must give up what you are.'

Cancer was the messenger to help me realise how far from living in integrity with my true self I had travelled. It has forced me to peel back the layers of protection, distortion and adaptation, to feel each layer with its painful consequences and cost to my freedom. It's taken hard work, much forgiveness and is still a tender work in progress. It has revealed the diamond at my core. She was there all along, sparkling her magnificence beneath the caked on layers, just waiting for me to remember her.

Cancer is the gift that helped me to mine my diamond and re-discover the essence of who I truly am. I now shine in the full expression of my soul's truth and that has been cancer's greatest gift of all.

LOVE IN ACTION

INNER PRACTICE

Giving Gratitude

Giving thanks for what is present is one way of building our capacity to receive. It takes our attention away from a sense of lack, loss or scarcity and shifts our focus toward the abundance we already have. Noticing what we already have is a great way to create ease and harmony in our body and it really settles the nervous system. It is one of my favourite practices.

Practicing an attitude of gratitude is therapeutic in itself. It is a medicine you share with yourself and with others. It is more powerful than we know and a fabulous remedy to raise our vibrational frequency.

Write down all of the abundance present in your life, small and large.

What are you grateful for at this moment?

Consider voicing your gratitude to the heavens or to those people for whom you are grateful.

OUTER PRACTICE
Sacred Self Care

Sacred self-care is the ultimate act of self-love. It's about carving out precious time to get to know yourself more intimately, understand your needs more fully and learn to honour all parts of yourself. How we relate to and care for ourselves ripples through every part of our body, our being and our life.

Throughout my treatment journey, I was absolutely 100% committed to finding ways to honour my body and encourage restoration and repair. I found plenty of ways to introduce sacred self-care as I had given little time to myself before. Here are some of the ways I now practice regular self-care:

Quality foods – I believe much of our health stems from the quality of foods we eat. For years I thought I 'deserved' that glass of vino or big piece of chocolate cake like they were some kind of treat but in reality, nourishing my body and soul with healthy, organic, wholefoods has been far more beneficial in the long run. For some of the recipes that helped me survive chemo and many others that I have found along the way that are not only delicious, but nutritious, visit www.healingjournal.co.

Naturopathy – As you would know by now, I had HUGE resistance to receiving chemotherapy and Herceptin infusions and would have preferred to treat my cancer with more natural methods. Instead, I opted for a west meets east approach and sought the advice and support of two naturopaths. Erin and Greg were instrumental in helping me to manage side effects, support gut health, digestive and liver function and maintain optimal health through natural therapies like teas, oils, supplements and mindfulness practices.

Massage – My body has always responded well to touch and seems to be a natural way to instruct my muscles to relax and release tension. One of the things I absolutely committed to throughout treatment was receiving a weekly massage, two if I could manage it. I varied the types of massage and found lymphatic drainage, kahuna, Zen-thai shiatsu or any relaxation massage was essential to my coping and recovery.

Acupuncture – This ancient medicine originating in China is believed to restore flow and balance to our life force energy through the insertion of small needles into various pressure points around our body. I have personally found acupuncture to be very beneficial and incorporated this into my weekly schedule. Be sure to work with a practitioner who is properly trained.

Essential Oils – I love essential oils and have incorporated them into my daily life. They help me to evoke different emotional states depending on what I need at the time. I use them in a multitude of ways; I often have a diffuser burning, add oils to my bath, roll oil blends onto my skin, mist oils onto my face or use in my Aromatic Self-Love Ritual as below.

Aromatic Self Love Ritual – I created this ritual to carve out time each day to honour myself with a full mind and body treatment. It is one of the greatest insurance policies for overall health. It only takes about two minutes so it's perfect even on the busiest of days.

I like to do this ritual following my morning shower:

1. Start by asking yourself 'How do I feel?' I find this simple check-in acknowledging my body and how I feel is a powerful way to set myself up for a great day.
2. Then select the appropriate synergy blend of oils to support that feeling. Essential oils are magical and can change the way you feel in just seconds.
3. You will need: your favourite essential oils, massage base-oil (I like almond or apricot oil), a small bowl and your wonderful naked body.
4. Place a teaspoon of massage base-oil and three drops of your chosen essential oils into your dish.
5. Inhale the aroma.
6. Now let's wake up your body, starting at your feet. Work your way up each leg, honouring as you go, working up over the hips and around your buttocks. Move onto your tummy in a clockwise direction to support digestive function and up over the whole chest and breast area. Move up over your shoulders giving them a gentle squeeze to release any tension there. Then work down each arm into both hands.
7. Cup your hands over your face breathing in the beautiful aroma. Tell yourself how wonderful you are and create a mantra like 'I am strong', 'I am healing everyday' or 'I love and accept my body'. Ask yourself what you want more of in your life – and believe you will get it.
8. Repeat this daily. Your body is your temple. Honour it every day of your life.

Blissful Baths – I have always loved a warm bath. It is the perfect place to create a sanctuary with candles, magnesium salts and blissful oils, soulful music and I am in heaven. Add a few drops of your favourite oils. Check out some of my favourite recipes online or choose from those in the table, opposite.

Essential Oil Body Blends to Support Treatment

Here are some of my favourite go-to oils that have helped me through treatment.

INTENTION	HEALTH BENEFITS	RECOMMENDED OILS
Relaxation	Helps to relieve stress and promote calm + relaxation	Cedarwood, Bergamot Geranium, Lavender, Rosewood
Energise	Helps to relieve fatigue + lethargy + increase energy	Rosemary, Basil, Lemon, Lime, Black Pepper
Unwind	Helps to relieve symptoms of stress, headaches, fatigue + improve stability + grounding	Bergamot, Neroli, Frankincense, Lavender, Sandalwood, Geranium
Sensuality	Enhances loving relationships, intimacy, romance + positive communication	Ylang Ylang, Orange, Patchouli, Sandalwood
Clarity	Helps to become more focused with clarity + inspiration	Basil, Rosemary, Lemon, Rosewood, Pine
Peace	To help create a sense of calm, peace + tranquillity	Frankincense, Orange, Pine, Lavender, Sandalwood
Serenity	Helps to strengthen an overburdened nervous system + restore calm	Lavender, Chamomile, Orange, Neroli, Frankincense, Cypress
Immunity	Stimulates the body's ability to fight off stress related illnesses, headaches + flus	Eucalyptus, Lavender, Cedarwood, Cypress, Lime, Tea Tree
Balance	Helps to bring balance to hormone fluctuations	Chamomile, Clary Sage, Jasmine, Lavender, Geranium

Drinking Tea – Tea has been called the plant of Heaven. For 4000 years, it's been valued both as a medicine and drink for pleasure.

I love to create rituals around everyday things like doing EFT with an affirmation in the shower (see pg 206), writing down what I'm grateful for in a special diary every night in bed and drinking tea to create an intentional pause to rest throughout my day. Tea has many healing properties and is a beautiful way to honour yourself. Ginger tea was particularly helpful in coping with the side effects of chemo. Select your chosen tea from the table below or visit my website for some of my favourite blends to specifically address managing the symptoms of chemotherapy and radiation.

Tea Varieties

VARIETY OF TEA	BENEFIT
Chamomile	Soothing, sleep inducing tea
Fennel	Helpful tea for digestion
Ginger	Supports digestion, immunity + circulation
Rooibos	Useful for headaches, restlessness, allergies + hypertension
Peppermint	A refreshing tea that is cooling + settles and upset stomach
Tulsi or 'Holy Basil'	Great for strengthening our energy reserves
Licorice	Aids digestion + soothes the stomach
Lemon Myrtle	Helpful with headaches, colds + flu
Rosehip	Vibrant tea loaded with antioxidants, vitamin C + disease fighting compounds
White	Wonderful for glowing skin + general health maintenance
Chai	Warming, spicy tea cherished for preserving health + peace of mind
Green	Rich in antioxidants for health + beauty

When I drink tea
I am conscious of peace
The cool breath of Heaven
rises in my sleeves and
blows my cares away.

— CHINESE POET LUNG

Drink Tea

Zenchi - One of the things that I discovered along my journey is a machine called a Zenchi. I was very sceptical about its many suggested benefits but thought I would give it a try. I was carrying a great deal of pain in my bones and muscles so I was willing to try anything that might give me comfort.

The vibrational movement created by the Zenchi is said to free up blocked energy and enhance the feeling of wellbeing. It is designed to stimulate venous and lymphatic return, release muscular tension and have an overall effect on the digestive process. It sounded like the perfect solution so I gave it a try. I fell in love with this little gem and introduced a 20-minute session with my Zenchi into my morning ritual.

Forest Bathing - I love walking along the beach but I think I love walking in the forest even more. I guess that's the Canadian in me! Have you ever stopped and touched a tree? What did it feel like?

Time in nature has been one of the most helpful ways to help ground me and bring serenity when I least felt it. I aim to walk in nature several times a week.

What are the self-care practices that nurture and restore you?

Am I willing to fully accept myself with all my imperfections?

In what ways could I love and care for myself more?

How could I simplify my life to make space for those things I wish to honour more fully?

Where do I experience love in my life? How does it feel?

What gifts have I received from this journey?

What gifts do I now have to offer as a result of this journey?

Joy

Thank You Sister

I hope the time you have spent reflecting, going inward to hear your own wisdom, has deepened your journey through cancer treatment and beyond.

I hope you have taken this opportunity to explore what may lie at the root of your cancer so you can make changes that support you in your life. I want you to live your brightest, most beautiful life from now on.

Even though I can't be with you, please know that I am walking alongside you in spirit, and know that you are held in Divine Love. I believe in you and have faith that you can do this.

Unfortunately, it is statistically very likely that many of us will encounter this unwanted visitor, cancer, if not in our own life, in those close to us. We have so much to learn from each other. Please share this *Healing Journal*, with every woman whose life is touched by cancer. It is my hope and intent that this journal acts as a big nurturing hug and a helpful guide when we need it most.

Proceeds from this book will go to organisations that are actively researching the cause and ultimate cure for cancer so that we can live in a world that is cancer-free. That change starts with each of us. Women coming into our power, creating agency within our own lives, building a brighter future, speaking our truth and helping each other to heal.

It is my dream that this book finds its way into the hands and hearts of every woman touched by cancer; that it supports, encourages, inspires and empowers them in every way they need it. And that it activates powerful, positive healing and transformation, in all the ways they dream of.

From my heart to yours.

With so much gratitude,

Cindy Scott xx

THERE COMES A POINT WHERE WE NEED TO STOP JUST PULLING PEOPLE OUT OF THE RIVER.

We need to go upstream and find out why they're falling in.

- Archbishop Desmond Tutu

WILD GEESE

You do not have to be good.
You do not have to walk on your knees
For a hundred miles through the desert, repenting.
You only have to let the soft animal of your body
Love what it loves.
Tell me about your despair, yours, and I will tell you mine.
Meanwhile the world goes on.
Meanwhile the sun and the clear pebbles of rain
Are moving across the landscape,
Over the prairies and the deep trees,
The mountains and the rivers.
Meanwhile the wild geese, high in the clean blue air,
Are heading home again.
Whoever you are, no matter how lonely,
The world offers itself to your imagination,
Calls to you like the wild geese, harsh and exciting…
Over and over announcing your place
In the family of things.

- Mary Oliver

TELL ME,
*what is it
you plan to do
with your one
wild & precious
life?*

- Mary Oliver

So Much Gratitude

It takes a community of people to support a woman through her cancer journey. I have so much gratitude for the many people that touched my life through this most challenging time. There are so many who supported me, too many to mention here but I hope they know who they are. These people in particular I want to acknowledge:

My parents: Carl and Glenda Turner for your continuous contact, concern and support.

My Aussie family: John, Anne + Jo Page for your ongoing presence, love and compassion.

My mother-in-law: Dawn Scott whose compassion and support made me feel so held and loved. Dawn read this manuscript and offered her valuable and honest feedback.

Danni Crocker, my fairy friend who is simply the most loving, kind and generous soul who held my hand through all of the good and bad.

Erin Quint for walking alongside me and giving me her wise, naturopathic counsel, friendship and very generous support.

Merryn Penington for her incredible zen-thai shiatsu bodywork, healing vibes and timely wisdom throughout my journey.

My medical team for getting me here.

Doctors: Dr Paula Fukuda Pissini, Dr Emma Secomb, Dr Hong Shue, Dr Emilia Dauway
Nurses: Kathy Apelt, Christine, Gabrielle, Dan, Melissa, Amelia, Jenny and the team at Sunshine Coast Haematology and Oncology Centre (SCHOC)
Psychologists: Keely Gordon-King, Tracey Young
Naturopaths: Erin Quint, Greg Fredericks

The Cancer Council, Bloomhill Cancer Care and Cindy Mackenzie Breast Cancer Program for their support.

My soul sisters for our weekly zoom calls throughout the year.

Our calls kept me grounded, connected and sane through the most challenging time of my life. I will be forever grateful for your unwavering support and compassion through my darkest hours and time of most need. Michelle Adams, Benay Dyor, Erin Lee and Lisa Whiting.

The gorgeous, wise and beautiful women and men whom I've leaned on and woven into this book:

Jill Chivers, Vida Carlino, Leonie Lomax, Merryn Penington, Erin Quint, Benay Dyor and her daughter Mya, Gail McCane, Stacy Phillips, Bart Kok + Josh Gardner

The generous souls whose valuable contribution made this book possible:

Leonie Lomax
Rachelle Thomas
Cathryn Lloyd
Melody Jansz
Julie Drechsler
Paula Mack
Louise + Gary Lamont
John + Anne Page
Jennifer Clarke
Megan Vuillermin
Joanne Page
Lyn Hawkins
Vincent Wellink
Ange + Marcel Leclerc
Kylie Riley

Tim Marchington
Enna Giampiccolo
Tania + Glyn Wakeman
Venetia Rodrigues
Carl + Glenda Turner
Dawn Scott
Justine Potter
Pat + Paul Lonergan
Tracey Maree
Danielle Bolton
Dr Emilia Dauway
Rhonda + Tom Kerr
Ashley + Brenda Bonner
Robyn Dodd
Dominique Davidson

Michele O'Brien
Pat Mosher
Shelley + Paul Nowlan
Chantal Roelofs
Tracey + Steve Gibson
Di + Ian Thomas
Toni Kneebone
Debs + David Cuthill
Jacque Rice
Wendy Barnes
Mel Daniels
Trish + Lenny Merrett
Tracey + Steve Gibson
Di Mills
Chris Astbury

References &
RECOMMENDED READING

Benson, Herbert M.D. & Klipper, Miriam Z., 2000, *The Relaxation Response,* William Morrow

Brackett, Marc, 2019, *Permission to Feel: Unlocking the Power of Emotions to Help Our Kids, Ourselves, and Our Society Thrive,* Celadon Books

Brown, Brené, 2012, *Daring Greatly: How the Courage to be Vulnerable Transforms the Way We Live, Love, Parent and Lead,* Penguin

Brown, Brené, 2010, *The Gifts of Imperfection, Let Go Of Who You Think You're Supposed To Be and Embrace Who You Are,* Hazelden

Chodron, Pema, 2016, *When Things Fall Apart: Heart Advice for Difficult Times,* Shambhala

Chopra, Deepak & Tanzi, Rudolph E., 2018, *The Healing Self: Supercharge Your Immune System and Stay Well For Life,* Ebury Digital

Dalla-Camina, Megan, 2019, *Simple, Soulful, Sacred: A Woman's Guide to Clarity, Comfort and Coming Home to Herself,* Hay House

Dauway, Emilia M.D., 2020, *Live Fearlessly: Liberating Your Life After Breast Cancer,* Emilia Dauway

Dispenza, Joe M.D., 2014, *You Are The Placebo: Making Your Mind Matter,* Hay House

Dispenza, Joe M.D., 2012, *Breaking The Habit of Being Yourself: How to Lose Your Mind and Create a New One,* Hay House

Duerk, Judith, 2004, *Circle of Stones: Woman's Journey to Herself,* New World Library

Frankl, Viktor, 2011, *Man's Search for Meaning,* Rider

Hanson, Rick, 2009, *Buddha's Brain: The Practical Neuroscience of Happiness, Love, and Wisdom,* New Harbinger

Hay, Louise, 2004, *You Can Heal Your Life,* Hay House

Kabat-Zinn, Jon, 2005, *Wherever You Go, There You Are,* Hatchett Books

Lipton, Bruce H. Ph.D., 2005, *The Biology of Belief: Unleashing the Power of Consciousness, Matter & Miracles,* Mountain of Love

Moorjani, Anita, 2012, *Dying To Be Me: My Journey From Cancer, To Near Death, To True Healing,* Hay House

Myss, Caroline, 2003, *Sacred Contracts: Awakening Your Divine Potential,* Harmony

Neff, Kristin Ph.D., 2011, *Self-Compassion: The Proven Power of Being Kind to Yourself,* HarperCollins

Rankin, Lissa M.D., 2013, *Mind Over Medicine: Scientific Proof That You Can Heal Yourself,* Hay House

Segal, Inna, 2010, *The Secret Language of Your Body: The Essential Guide to Healing,* Atria Books

Turner, Toko-pa, 2017, *Belonging: Remembering Ourselves Home,* Her Own Room Press

Williamson Marianne, 1992, *A Return to Love: Reflections on the Principles of A Course in Miracles,* Harper Collins

My Health Records

This is a special section in this Journal for you to capture your own personal health records, your medical team, family history, your treatment journey and self-care practices. I found that it was tremendously helpful to have all of this information in one place.

MY HEALTH MANAGEMENT TEAM

Specialisation	Name	Contact Number
GP		
Surgeon		
Medical Oncologist		
Radiation Oncologist		
Dietician/Nutritionist		
Naturopath		
Psychologist		
Massage Therapist		
Exercise Physiologist		
Nurse		
Geneticist		
Nearest Hospital		
Other		

Date of Cancer Diagnosis

Cancer Type

Cancer Pathology

Genetic Profile

MY FAMILY HEALTH HISTORY

What's happening in my immediate family?

And my extended family? On my mothers side, and my father's side?

_____
_____
_____
_____
_____
_____
_____
_____

What do I know about the possible impact of my disease on my children?

_____
_____
_____
_____
_____
_____
_____
_____
_____

MY CLINICAL TREATMENTS
SURGERY

Date _____ Doctor _____ Location _____

Reflections... _____

_____

_____

_____

Date _____ Doctor _____ Location _____

Reflections... _____

_____

_____

_____

Date _____ Doctor _____ Location _____

Reflections... _____

_____

_____

_____

You are braver than you believe,
Stronger than you seem,
Smarter than you think,
And loved more than you'll ever know.

- A.A. MILNE
From the book *WINNIE THE POOH*

MY CHEMOTHERAPY TREATMENTS

Doctor _____ Location of Treatment _____

Date _____ Medication _____

Reflections/Comments... _____

_____

_____

_____

Date _____ Medication _____

Reflections/Comments... _____

_____

_____

_____

Date _____ Medication _____

Reflections/Comments... _____

_____

_____

_____

Date _____ Medication _____

Reflections/Comments... _____

_____

_____

_____

Date   Medication

Reflections/Comments...

Date   Medication

Reflections/Comments...

Date   Medication

Reflections/Comments...

Date   Medication

Reflections/Comments...

Date _____ Medication _____

Reflections/Comments...

Date _____ Medication _____

Reflections/Comments...

Date _____ Medication _____

Reflections/Comments...

Date _____ Medication _____

Reflections/Comments...

Date _____ Medication _____
Reflections/Comments...

Date _____ Medication _____
Reflections/Comments...

Date _____ Medication _____
Reflections/Comments...

Date _____ Medication _____
Reflections/Comments...

MY RADIATION TREATMENTS

Doctor _____ Area Radiated _____

Date _____ Reflections/Comments _____

_____

_____

Date _____ Reflections/Comments... _____

_____

_____

Date _____ Reflections/Comments... _____

_____

_____

Date _____ Reflections/Comments... _____

_____

_____

Date _____ Reflections/Comments... _____

_____

_____

Date	Reflections/Comments

Date	Reflections/Comments...

Date	Reflections/Comments...

Date	Reflections/Comments...

Date	Reflections/Comments...

Date _____ Reflections/Comments _____

Date _____ Reflections/Comments... _____

Date _____ Reflections/Comments... _____

Date _____ Reflections/Comments... _____

Date _____ Reflections/Comments... _____

Date _____ Reflections/Comments _____

Date _____ Reflections/Comments... _____

Date _____ Reflections/Comments... _____

Date _____ Reflections/Comments... _____

Date _____ Reflections/Comments... _____

COMPLEMENTARY TREATMENTS

SELF-CARE PRACTICES
How am I caring for myself?

HORMONE THERAPY & SUBSEQUENT TREATMENT

First published in 2021 by Cindy Scott

© Cindy Scott 2021

The moral rights of the author have been asserted.

All rights reserved. Except as permitted under the Australian Copyright Act 1968, no part of this book may be reproduced, stored in a retrieval system, communicated or transmitted in any form or by any means without prior written permission.

All inquiries should be made to the author.

ISBN: 978-0-646-83094-0

Printed in China on woodfree paper

Cover design by Melissa Williams

Internal layout and design by Stephanie Crane

Cover image provided by DepositPhotos

Disclaimer: The material in this publication is of the nature of general comment only, and does not represent professional advice. It is not intended to provide specific guidance for particular circumstances and it should not be relied on as the basis for any decision to take action or not take action on any matter which it covers. Readers should obtain professional advice where appropriate, before making any such decision. To the maximum extent of the law, the author and publisher disclaim all responsibility and liability to any person, arising directly or indirectly from any person taking or not taking action based on the information in this publication.